ORGANIZING FOR COMMUNITY ACTION

SAGE HUMAN SERVICES GUIDES, VOLUME 27

SAGE HUMAN SERVICES GUIDES

a series of books edited by ARMAND LAUFFER and published in cooperation with the University of Michigan School of Social Work.

A **SAGE** HUMAN SERVICES GUIDE **27**

ORGANIZING FOR COMMUNITY ACTION

SCHOOL OF
CALIFORNIA
PROFESSIONAL
PSYCHOLOGY
LOS ANGELES

Steve ⎣BURGHARDT

*Published in cooperation with the University of Michigan
School of Social Work*

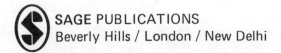

SAGE PUBLICATIONS
Beverly Hills / London / New Delhi

For information address:

SAGE Publications, Inc.
275 South Beverly Drive
Beverly Hills, California 90212

SAGE Publications India Pvt. Ltd.
C-236 Defence Colony
New Delhi 110 024, India

SAGE Publications Ltd
28 Banner Street
London EC1Y 8QE, England

Printed in the United States of America

Library of Congress Cataloging in Publication Data

Burghardt, Steve.
    Organizing for community action.

    (Sage human services guides ; v. 27)
    "Published in cooperation with the University of
Michigan School of Social Work."
    Bibliography: p.
    1. Community organization—United States.   2. Social
workers—United States—Political activity.   I. Title.
II. Series
HV65.B82   1982   361.2'5   82-6034
ISBN 0-8039-0206-9 (pbk.)

SECOND PRINTING, 1983

Dedicated with love and gratitude
to
Elizabeth R. Burghardt and Marshall Burghardt

CONTENTS

PREFACE

If you are a human service worker in the 1980s, you probably have considered becoming politically active in ways that you might never have considered before: signing petitions with your staff and community members on concerns of agency retrenchment, getting out votes on important issues in the legislative arena, or joining in an occasional demonstration or march to let people in Washington or your state capital know that people still want and need human services. It has almost become common for a large number of human service workers to engage in such actions, for the simple purpose of survival—of your job, your agency, entitlements, or programs you believe in. What once seemed to be the singular domain of the tenant organizer or community activist is today the world of the caseworker, health technician, and teacher. As a group worker recently put it, "It seems as though Ronald Reagan is bringing us together in ways no one else ever could before!"

Whatever your human service occupation, the dawning reaction to today's rightward currents demand that we all be familiar with the technqiues of grass-roots organizing. Such techniques emphasize our one undiminished resource: people and their individual and collective talents. The more we know how to use these talents, the stronger our cause can be. While you may not want a tenants' union, you can use some of their mobilizing tactics to build a strong support base to keep your agency in operation. If your mental health staff is not familiar with putting out leaflets for a rally to save jobs, then the skills picked up by school board activists can help.

In short, the increasingly common cause across all the human services today, to maintain and improve services, makes the grass-roots literature vital to our effectiveness, especially as other, more traditional approaches are undercut. This book, by drawing on the vast array of techniques presented throughout the grass-roots literature, seeks to make that common cause more effectively united by explaining those techniques as clearly and as concisely as possible. Whatever your organizational experience or area of service, this book can help you organize around the issues that are affecting you—right now.

This book came about for two reasons. First, Armand Lauffer, general editor of the Sage Human Services Guides, has long had a commitment to all areas of community organization and planning, and recognized the importance of a book on grass-roots organizing in the series. Second, having learned so much from so many others in my own experiences an an organizer over the past fifteen years, I wanted to put on paper what has changed since the 1960s in the ways grass-roots organizers do our work. What follows is a description of many of those changes, written especially for new organizers and other human service practitioners new to grass-roots work who recognize they must be active in the 1980s if their programs and communities are to survive. Its emphasis is on the mechanics of doing the work, spelling out political issues only as they influence those techniques. Broader political issues related to the content of the particular issues before us (from abortion rights to trade unionism) are not part of this book's domain. They do need to be addressed, but one should use other vehicles to do so.

I wish to extend my gratitude to countless numbers of people who have influenced and changed my life for the better—from those committed activists of the student and antiwar left of the late 1960s to the trade union and community coalition activists with whom I have been involved in New York since the onslaught of the city crisis. They did not write the book—they *are* the book.

Besides Armand Lauffer, I wish to thank Bibi Gafar for her assistance in the manuscript's preparation, and Phyllis Caroff, Irwin Esptein, Michael Fabricant, Joel Walker, and Harold Weissman for the moral support they gave as the writing went on. Finally, I especially thank Paula Kramer and Lila Kramer-Burghardt for all the Good Company.

INTRODUCTION

Grass-roots organizing, contrary to much popular opinion, has been an active, diversified phenomenon thoughout the 1970s and early 1980s.[1] Men and women from every walk of life have developed groups, planned strategies, determined tactics, and pressured political leaders on issues as far-ranging as nuclear power, neighborhood services, women's rights, working conditions, and gentrification. And the numbers get larger every day.

This is especially true for human service workers. People who never thought of themselves as "organizers" have been out fighting for causes they believe in and programs they wish to keep. Be it the caseworker working for the ERA or the hospital worker fighting alongside others to keep a local hospital open, human service workers are becoming involved more today than at any time since the 1960s.

Many of the tactics and short-term strategies are remarkably innovative, showing real growth in sophistication and awareness over the last ten years, we shall see. But there is a difference—a big difference—between the organizing of today and that of the 1960s, when many of the present organizing models were developed. In the 1960s, people marched and dreams were, if not fulfilled, at least believed in; in the 1980s we march less, and when we do, it is often to keep nightmares from happening. The cold, hard reality to our organizing in the 1980s is that we are often on the defensive; it is the Right that has the power and momentum to achieve much of its agenda and attain *its* dreams—dreams that do not include community organizers, human service workers, working people, and the poor except, as irritants to be ignored, or, better, made available for the harsher working and living conditions demanded by our presumably depleted economy.

Facing this defensive reality may seem like an odd way to begin a book on grass-roots organizing. After all, aren't we supposed to be upbeat, building people's spirits, working in ways to make them feel like more is possible, that with a little more effort we can all succeed? My experience with this approach to organizing—where the organizer "ego boosts" the "community folks" in overstated terms so they will stay active for the long haul—is that it is both manipulative and condescending. Instead, a good organizer—one who works *with* people to develop strategies with short-term tactical effectiveness and long-term political potential—begins with two fundamental assumptions that make this work politically meaningful and personally rewarding.

First, we must really trust that people, given genuine alternatives, will act with decency, humanity, and skill. This may sound trite, but it is not, as Paulo Freire has noted again and again.[3] Many organizers prefer to work *for* "the people." They often are highly progressive politically in terms of *issues.* They fight for decent housing for all, child care on an as-needed basis, and an end to all forms of racism and sexism. But they do the work with disregard for the people themselves, trusting only their ability to get the work done; that is, for all their egalitarian commitment, they may feel that only they are smart enough and skilled enough for the really important jobs (speaking before *large* gathering, addressing the politicians, and so on). Such lack of trust, carried to its logical end, means that at best the hands of power, not its shape, will change. Changing the shape of power is what good grass-roots organizers try to do, but they must begin by trusting people for such change to be possible. If you do not believe this, you will display the "false generosity" Freire condemns in manipulators and users of people.[4] If you do believe it—or at least are willing to work towards it—manipulation and dishonest posturing for short-term effect seems to disappear.

Second, every strategy must be based on some sound objective that corresponds to the actual conditions and perceptions of people's lives. I have been part of too many groupings with good potential that fell apart because of all the woulds, coulds, shoulds, and musts that permeated the groups' atmosphere. People need to believe that justice is on their side, but that's quite different from assuming one's degree of justice (or level of oppression) is an automatic lever to power. We all need to work with our perceptions of justice *and* our actual resources in whatever form we find them to keep a group active and engaged. Today we are usually strong on the former and a bit weak in the latter, while in the 1960s the mix was a more even, headier brew. However, while our numbers initially will not approach thos of the past, people today can accept the present blend if it still allows for forward momentum. That means we begin from an admittedly defensive position—one that in its openness respects people enough to share that reality while, at the same time, giving us ample opportunity to measure success in terms that in previous years would not have been acceptable or understood.

You will notice that I said "or understood" as well as "acceptable." To have written "acceptable" alone would have furthered one of the increasingly romanticized myths of the 1960s, namely, that 1960s organizing should be the political and organizational standard by which all our efforts are measured. In fact, there were more than a few major strategic errors in that period that are still embedded in many approaches to organizing. One of the most blatant was the complete inattention to the personal needs and interests of the individuals involved, which not only ignored a large segment of people's lives but helped create and perpetuate an elitist model of organizing—one usually dominated by white males.[5] In the long run, of course, such an approach burnt out most organizers before they were thirty, forcing many—especally Blacks, Latinos, and women—to cut back their actions because they needed to address demands in their personal lives left unattended because of their organizing efforts.[6]

Furthermore, as members of the women's movement have so amply pointed out, most organizing strategies of the 1960s assumed that only the *content* of an issue mattered, not the form and manner of how one organized. For example, Saul Alinsky gave eloquent, cynical testimony of such an approach in his famous "On Means and Ends" chapter in *Rules for Radicals*.[7] He essentially argued that victors determined morality, not the reverse. While the issues of power Alinsky discussed need to be understood historically, the political logic of his argument (written with the kind of bravado common to too many male organizers) justified almost any line of attack as long as it was successful.[8] Such an analysis, like so many of that period, ignores the role played by organizers and activists either in *re-creating* similar forms of leadership and organization (which thus carry little threat to existing *institutional relations*) or in *creating* new forms of collective leadership and organization (which, however small, may carry the threatening seeds of genuine change in those relationships). By emphasizing content to the exclusion of process, the organizing models of the 1960s, for all their militancy, too often created similar models of hierarchical practice that posed little threat to the established institutional order. This book, while developed in a period of far more defensive activity, will try to correct that error.

Organizing for Community Action will therefore attempt to interlace three primary themes through its chapters. *First, the tactical discussions of each chapter flow out of the strategic assumption that*

*community and social service activists are currently working in a
defensive context.* That context can shift quickly, of course, but there
is little on the political horizon of the 1980s that suggests any rapid
transformation to wide-scale, surging progressive movements of social
change. Here this means that tactics will be grounded in ways that
help us maintain needed momentum without losing sight of either our
present power base (limited) or our inherent potential for the future
(much greater).

That we work within a defensive context does not mean we work
defensively; far from it. *It means working realistically, working with
and respecting the personal and political strengths and limitations
of our members and organizations as they are and not as we wish
them to be.* By developing a series of well-orchestrated tactics, from
initial preplanning to calls for action and beyond, which show respect
for people and what can be accomplished—letting them develop their
skills and determine targets in *their* terms—you begin to move toward
the kind of work that is achievable and yet implicitly goes beyond present assumptions of power.

All of this speaks to the third theme of this book, one that tries to
correct some of the errors of the past: *that the way we perform our
tasks is in fact a highly political act,* for its manner can create a set of
working relationships that are deeply opposed to present procedures:
collective rather than individual leaders; the joining of personal and
political concerns rather than pulling them apart; the emphasis on
"common folk" determining for themselves rathern than being determined by. Such an emphasis makes it possible to draw political satisfaction from our work even when our overall strategic success re-
mains limited. For in the alteration of how we work, even on small
tasks, are the elements of a world far different from what we have now,
and *that* is the real dream of every progressive organizer.

The outline of this book, however, emphasizes the clear operational
organizing needs of human service workers, not lofty dreams. The
flow of the work is sequential; therefore the book creates a model of an
activist group going through and completing all stages of expansion
and change. At the same time, the emphasis on descriptive techniques
will make it possible for the reader to jump from chapter to chapter,
using the book on an "as-needed" basis. Thus, a human service
worker wanting to hold a meeting at his or her workplace can turn to
Chapter 4 without reading the chapters before it.

Each chapter will begin not with a major strategic problem but with
a description of one of the most common practitioner concerns or

fears concerning the chapter's particular organizing issue. For example, many new organizers are terrified at the thought of speaking in public. Often this is because they have an image of a great orator whom they could never emulate; others believe they must adopt a particular speaking style foreign to their background. I shall deal directly with these fears—concerns that undercut tactical effectiveness, regardless of political commitment—and spell out a number of techniques one can use to learn how to speak clearly and effectively. At the end of each chapter there will be different exercises to help the reader develop tactical skill as quickly as possible.

The book is designed primarily for two groups: (1) human service workers who are new to organizing and who may feel the tasks are "too big" for them to handle; (2) people who, after a 1970s lull, are returning to organizing, wonder what they need to "brush up" on, and are a little uncertain (correctly so) about applying techniques last used during, say, an antiwar march in 1971.

As mentioned, the work is sequential, moving from the preplanning stages, where general political orientations are thought through (Introduction and Chapter 1), understanding individual and group needs (Chapters 2 and 3), to learning the varying routines of daily organizing and how to run meetings that are important for an organization's development (Chapters 4 and 5), expanding outward in actions that involve other groups and organizations (Chapters 6 and 7), and evolving ways a group can maximize the potential for both internal democracy and eradicating vestiges of racism, sexism, and class bias. A final chapter on how to analyze organizing tasks for the 1980s is included to stimulate the reader to go beyond tactical considerations. An annotated bibliography on good organizing literature, a list of organizing institutes and centers, and organizing newsletters are included for the reader to use in his or her ongoing work as a resource.

NOTES

1. For evidence of how widespread the activity has been, see Harry Boyte, *The Backyard Revolution* (Philadelphia: Temple University Press, 1981).

2. Such distinctions will be clarified in the first chapter.

3. Paulo Freire, *Pedagogy of the Oppressed* (New York: Seabury Press, 1972). This book on "revolutionary pedagogy" is a must for anyone working in community or social service practice.

4. Freire, *Pedagogy,* p. 47.

5. For an excellent critique of the dominant 1960s model, see Kathy McAley and City Life, "From the Movements," in *Radical America,* Fall 1978.

6. For a more thorough theoretical discussion of how to join the "personal and political" into one's organizing strategy, see Steve Burghardt, *The Other Side of Organizing* (Cambridge, MA: Schenkman, 1981).

7. Saul Alinsky, *Rules for Radicals* New York: Random House, 1967).

8. The work also implicitly justified the status quo, as Alinsky's discussion took place in terms of only major institutions and dominant actors. The idea that certain approaches that appealed to and were based on an *unyielding principle* of mobilization and genuine popular participation was never considered by Alinsky. The masses were mobilized for demonstrations, not decision making.

Chapter 1

PLANNING FOR GRASS-ROOTS ACTIVITY

Most new organizers are nervous about two things when they embark on an organizing drive: first, that they will make fools of themselves by being too obviously ignorant of and unskilled in the subject with which they are supposed to be dealing; second, that whatever they do, however small, will mean *something*—will accomplish something that improves people's lives. The first fear will be discussed in the Chapter 2. All that need be said here is that *all* organizers make mistakes and need to know more; the only thing to feel foolish about is the fear of admitting that such mistakes do happen.

The second, political concern is the topic of this chapter. A strategy that improves people's lives must, despite all the nice phrases, be rooted in politics, either explicitly or implicitly. After all, a need for improvement means that social conditions are not all they should be, although those who control those conditions may often disagree. However, by "politics" I do not mean "electoral politics," but a set of beliefs about four strategically important questions: (1) How is society controlled and how does it function? (2) What are the nature and causes of social problems? (3) Who should participate and determine how those problems are dealt with? (4) What are the appropriate vehicles to use in correcting those problems? Your answers to those questions are political; you will encounter those who disagree with those answers who therefore will seek to keep you from being effective. This is what strategy is all about: the creation of a plan that in someway challenges, debates, and acts to resolve differences in a group's favor. Such a process is the essence of politics. (The exercise at the end of the chapter can help orient you to where you most likely stand on these issues, locating you in terms of the three ideological groups discussed below.)

Of course, many organizers and activists do not act with conscious political intentions. A human service worker, for example, may want to save a hospital or keep a center open in the evenings for teens—to help his or her community, in other words. This was certainly how I began as an organizer, trying to form a tutorial program for poor children in the mid-1960s. But I soon learned, at first by trial and error (many errors), later by hard knocks (many knocks), and later by serious study, that this approach is impossible to maintain for long.

This is impossible because the same tactic can be used for very different ends by people with very different political beliefs and goals. Depending on your beliefs about the four questions listed above, an activist may view different tactical demands (like who should be on the negotiating committee to help keep a hospital open) in very different terms. Likewise, for one activist a rent strike may simply be a fight against one bad landlord, while for another it is a far deeper political issue. The same tactic will therefore be used and analyzed quite differently by these two people. There is nothing wrong with this; there is no "wrong" or "right" resolution of such differences. But it must emanate from the activities of people directly affected by the choices made. Therefore, while an organizer may engage in similar tactics for years, he or she must understand the three levels on which every strategy functions: (1) its ideological level; (2) its strategic level; and (3) its tactical level.

THE IDEOLOGICAL LEVEL

The ideological level relates to a general set of beliefs regarding the previous four issues (nature of society, causes of social problems, who participates, and vehicles for change). These general principles can be broken into specific strategic and tactical issues, as Jack Rothman did in the late 1960s.[1] At one ideological extreme is a group like Italy's Red Brigade, who view the economic and political system as so corrupt that the major actors are impossible to work with and must be destroyed. They therefore use terrorism as a vehicle to create upheavel and eventual social revolution. At the opposite extreme would be an exclusive neighborhood association interested in charity bazaars for neighborhood beautification projects, whose members view discussion of more serious social problems as ungrateful, collective whining. In general, however, most organizers fall into three ideological groups: (1) reformers, (2) social democrats, and (3) Marxists.[2]

Reformers are usually either new to organizing or are professionals who consciously drop any ideological/political issue from their overt strategic discussion and instead *concentrate on the issue in terms of organizational strategy alone.* The issue of a systemwide critique is never raised, even though a segment of the system may be attacked (the auto industry, a community board, landlords, or the like). Furthermore, one's choice of allies and arenas in which to operate—from corporate board rooms to storefronts to electoral politics—is wide open. The strength in this ideological stance is that a wide audience and wide-scale activity are more easily attained; its weakness is that the reforms may prove hollow and, once achieved, may be easily undermined by others more ideologically prepared to wait out the reformers' zeal.

The social democratic approach, unlike the reformers', incorporates a consistent systemic critique of our economic and political system into its organizational strategies. In the main, *they view capitalism as a system that no longer works in its present form.* They therefore seek not its overthrow but its restructuring. Rebuilding the Democratic party, developing "economic democracy" in the workplace through worker participation on corporate boards, and creating alternative sources of energy are three hallmark examples of the social democratic approach. Social democratic organizational strategies are therefore consistently concerned with these issues of structural reform and work within institutions to improve them. The strengths of this approach are its telling critique of American society and the rational alternatives it offers; its weakness has been to gloss over the dynamics of power in institutions that historically have shown little internal motivation to change, especially in times of economic constraint.[3]

The *Marxists* are the third ideological group who, like the social democrats, share a systemic critique of our economic and political institutions. However, unlike social democrats, Marxists do not believe there is much long-term potential in the restructuring of our dominant institutions.[4] Thus, while perhaps willing to push certain reforms like economic democracy, they would do so with an eye to raising the limitations to this approach as well, posing a broad social transformation in the process (for example, "workers' control" versus "economic democracy"; a labor party as opposed to a reformed Democratic party). The Marxists' strategic emphasis is on working with important institutions like trade unions and labor-community coalitions; the approach stresses "independent political organization" (such as caucuses independent of trade union officials' control in unions) as its hallmark. Its great strength is its systemic critique and its ability to ferret out the weaknesses of other strategies; its weakness is its continuing marginality and limited support for its alternatives—alternatives not always well thought out.[5]

The reason for this brief discussion on the ideological level of strategic development is twofold. First, as an organizer you will eventually be confronted by people who will demand an accurate accounting of your beliefs—or who are politically sophisticated enough to tell you your ideology in ways that can be unnerving if you are not prepared. This is a defensive reason for becoming clear about your beliefs. The second one is more positive, however. By becoming ideologically clear, your belief system guides you, helping you to spot others' basic beliefs more easily, and to draw from that insight a better understanding of whom one can and cannot work with over time. In short, you stop *reacting* to events and become able to plan for them. Any belief system needs to be tested and changed, too, but its underpinnings can and will permeate much of what we do and how we do it. The greater its clarity, the stronger and more certain your strategic sense—even when strategic options are limited.

How do we develop such clarity? There are two simple principles: (1) study, and (2) testing that study through practice. There is no substitute for the hard work involved in reading, struggling with ideas, and then testing those ideas in action. There is no magical point at which organizers (or anybody else) arrive and—poof!—know enough to preclude reading more theoretical material that forces us to confront the limits to our practice. Likewise, no theory is so correct that its limits do not need to be tested consistently in practice. If you are really serious about being an organizer, there is no substitute for this ongoing mixture of building theory and practice.[6]

If you're uncertain how to begin such a process (especially on the theoretical side), simply approach someone you respect and ask for a brief reading list on an issue or problem *in which you are interested.* (Don't take a topic you feel you *should* know but really do not care about; you will find yourself reading the same pages ten times before giving up.) Make certain the reading list begins with some concrete issues and then extends to more theoretical material. Finally, do the reading with others in either a study group, a class (at either a traditional or a nontraditional school), or a political organization where the members have reached various levels of training and experience (new people bring insight and thoughtful questions unfettered by cant; experienced people give political depth and historical perspective).

THE STRATEGIC LEVEL

We work on our ideological beliefs throughout our lifetime, acknowledging that these beliefs permeate both our strategic choices and our day-to-day work. At the same time, immediate, practical concerns demand a lot of attention to strategic, organizational issues. *Strategy is different from tactics in that it is an overall plan of group and organizational development that sees its eventual goals in terms of a means-ends process,* where each tactic is both an end and a means to achieve the larger goals of the group.[7] For example, a rent strike is a very demanding, sophisticated *tactic* used to help develop a tenants' organization; its success is an end (or objective) in itself, but the manner and level of completion affect the eventual goal of a cohesive tenants' group.[8]

It is certainly easy enough to get tactics and strategy confused. The best way I have found to avoid confusion is by thinking of where the group wishes to be in a year and then breaking down tactical activity into more manageable, three-month units. For example, a group of us have been working to form a Human Services Activists' Network in New York. The group grew out of a late-1980 conference, where people identified their sense of personal and political isolation in their work, coupled with a sense of political frustration and lack of movement in the overall social welfare field.[9] Given this joint desire for greater political coherency and closer relationships with progressive activists, many of us who initiated this group hope that in a year's time it will have (1) a support base in at least fifteen to twenty-five agencies; (2) a network newsletter that is published periodically; and (3) a series of political workshops, coupled with some activity in a larger, citywide arena (such as one with formations fighting the Reagan cuts), that begins to suggest our modest, progressive presence in the city.

Such goals are too abstract to develop easily, especially as the group did not exist when such goals were imagined! Therefore, the *objectives* for the first three months were based on finding whether or not enough people would be interested in developing such a group. Accordingly, these objectives were more educational in nature, and tactical emphasis was on facilitating discussion, inviting people to discuss common issues and different perceptions on those issues, and *short* position papers. In three months one would hope to call for a broader-based group with a common proposal. We achieved this objective—one month late. Our tactical emphasis and objectives within this overall strategy allowed for group movement and personal satisfaction at the achievement of these three-month tasks. If we had used the *strategic* goals as our measurement, we would have ended up frustrated, demoralized, and probably less successful, since the frustration eventually would have surfaced in antagonistic, disruptive ways.

Thus, an organizer begins by thinking of strategies that can be implemented in manageable chunks of time, dividing that time into three-month tactical objectives. (You can do this for small details by the week, but don't become obsessive!) The easiest way to manage all of this is to buy a convenient unobstrusive notebook (mine is about six by nine inches) and divide it into sections (a section for telephone numbers, new contacts, and members; a section for each committee or task; a section for meeting plans and agendas; and so on).[10] At the beginning of the notebook, jot down your goals for a year from now. Under them list the objectives for the first three months. Then, in your calendar/date book, circle that three-month date and write "review of three-month objectives" as a reminder to you and the group to review progress, noting successes and problems and drawing up new objectives for the next three months. This guarantees efficiency and realistic strategic planning.

THE TACTICAL LEVEL

The tactics used in each three-month period will be of two kinds: what are commonly called process- and task-oriented tactics. Process-oriented tactics emphasize communication, dialogue, information sharing, and the manner in which things get done. Task-oriented tactics are concerned with concrete issues, action, and results. Neither is totally separable, of course, and many tactics can and will extend beyond any artificial three-month boundaries. Indeed, much of the ideological level of strategy is expressed through how you and the group separate out such tactical issues for work. Knowing when to emphasize process over task, and vice-versa, is one of the hardest jobs a group has, for the push to get things done always exists next to the pull to expand membership education and involvement.[11]

Three pivotal issues underline any discussion of tactics. First, *in what context is the group functioning?* In the early 1980s, most progressive community groups are on the defensive. They therefore have different objectives and a different pacing than groups of the 1960s, when vast mobilization and optimistic energy made for rapid group development and achievement. Tactics need to be fit to today's reality, so that their more modest objectives allow for success and continued momentum and avoid the defensiveness wrought by grandiose schemes guaranteed to fail.[12]

Second, *what are the actual resources at hand to achieve your objectives?* As stated in the Introduction, do not confuse the justice of your cause with your ability to win. You do use the issue of justice (or oppression, exploitation, and so on) as a resource to win popular support and increase membership activity, *but know your actual resource base in terms of numbers, money, types of skills (and accessibility to other organizations), and, above all, the time available to mount a campaign before choosing tactics.* A 1981 anti-Reagan demonstration sponsored by the major social welfare organizations and public-sector labor unions in New York was a colossal flop, because the organizers' boastful predictions of a 75,000-person turnout missed by about 72,500 people. An honest assessment of real resources, coupled with more modest expectations, would have been far more effective in the long run: the demonstrators would have avoided the defensiveness created through such a failure, a defensiveness that only helps others to continue working against them.

Third, are the tactics developed with people in their terms, so that the risks taken are understood and shared by everyone involved? This question partially reveals my own political stance, but I believe it is too important to ignore. Too many organizers design terrificly exciting tactics *for people,* who then are left to deal with the consequences of actions previously understood only in part. In such an approach, the young and/or job-secure organizer, steeped in political commitment rather than family debts, is willing to "sacrifice" herself or himself without realizing that others cannot afford such risks at that moment. If one really believes in bettering the lives of people, those people must be a part of the decisions that affect their lives. While it may mean we have to discuss certain actions (from recent strikes to job actions to school boycotts) in greater detail than we might like, there is no substitute for people being able to decide for themselves what risks to take. Once taken, the risks involved, because they have been understood, are more likely to be perceived as having been worth it, even if the tactics fail.[13] The reverse can also happen: Even if you succeed, often people do not care, because they did not participate in the decision-making on that action.

In conclusion, it is obvious that much goes into the preplanning of any grass-roots strategy: working toward ideological clarity to create overall strategic mooring for our tasks; developing strategies with operationally definable segments that can allow for successful growth and momentum even in difficult periods like today; learning how to think of tactics as part of a long means-ends chain that is realistic, productive, and politically consistent with the group's overall belief system. The next chapters will look at how an organizer, with others, actually develops these various tactical issues.

It is important to end this chapter on a personal note, one filled with political implications. As the foregoing strategic discussion suggests, grass-roots organizing can be both remarkably rewarding and difficult, challenging, and often exasperating work. As Chris Meagher, an activist lawyer working in the South Bronx, put it, "These problems come with the turf. Let's not kid ourselves. We do all this and suffer through things because we *want* to, not because we're heroes or martyrs." He was so right! We organizers do our work for ourselves as well as others; the strategic problems to be dealt with cannot be blamed on the people with whom we work. By admitting to the self-interest that underlies what we do, we free ourselves from potential condescension and the temptation to heap blame on those we are "helping" when the work does not go as well as expected. If that blaming occurs, it is time to look for other work. Honestly admit to the self-interest, accept the problems as the reaility of what organizing is, and it is far more likely you'll find the joys a lot more easily, too.

NOTES

1. Jack Rothman breaks these issues down into twelve different variables in his seminal organizing typology. See Jack Rothman, "Three Models of Community Organization Practice, Their Mixing and Phasing," in Cox et al. (eds.), *Strategies of Community Organization* (Itasca, IL: Peacock, 1979), pp. 25-45.

2. Within each grouping can be found "nationalists," those who choose to work only with one social grouping, such as Blacks, Latins, and women.

3. For examples of the strengths and weaknesses of a social democratic approach, see Michael Harrington, *The Twilight of Capitalism* (New York: Simon & Schuster, 1979) and Tom Hayden, *The American Future* (Boston: South End Press, 1980).

4. This is not to say that Marxists are opposed to working on reforms. With the exception of small groups of rigidly orthodox Marxists (who believe in pushing only "pure politics"), Marxists work on reforms not only to achieve them but to push the system to change even further, either by revealing to people institutional indifference to their plight (a radicalizing act) or to foster even better changes (a mobilizing act). The recent Polish upheaval, led by many revolutionaries, began over meat—as the Russian Revolution began over bread (and peace). See Rosa Luxenbourg, *Reform or Revolution?* (New York: International, 1967).

5. A magazine that captures this Marxist emphasis without being overly doctrinaire is *Against the Current* (New York: 45 West 10th St., Apt. 2-G). See also Paul Foote, *What Is Socialism?* (London: Pluto Press 1979).

6. A good theoretical synthesis of this mix is Paulo Freire, *Pedagogy of the Oppressed* (New York: Seabury Press, 1972); see also Karl Marx's *Theses on Feuerbach,* in *Karl Marx and Frederick Engels: Selected Works* (New York: International, 1968), pp. 28-30.

7. See Cox et al., *Strategies,* for an excellent reader on issues of strategy and tactics.

8. An example of how ideological beliefs would permeate this strategy might be that the reformer would work simply to build the organization through the strike; the social democrat and the Marxist would do the same, but would use strike issues to show the nature of property relations. That is, the former would look to quality public housing as a solution, the latter to continuing class struggle with tenants and workers to overthrow the entire system of property relations (even while perhaps supporting the call for public housing).

9. *Options for a Good Society: Visions from the Left* (New York: Columbia University, December 1980).

10. This may sound awfully minor, but it took me about five years to learn that my superior memory was given to terribly ineffective lapses that damaged my work. Furthermore, slips of paper and jottings on the back of books and newspapers get lost a lot more often than do larger, more sustantial-looking notebooks that contain your name, address, and phone number.

11. This issue will be discussed in greater detail throughout the book.

12. Remember, it is possible to have *a bold vision* of widespread, working-class activity—an ideological issue dealt with in terms of educational goals and group self-determination in its internal functioning—and *a modest tactical stance*—one that deals with extant objective conditions involving potential success, resources, and activity level.

13. See Freire, *Pedagogy,* pp. 47-77, for his brilliant discussion on "the helping process."

EXERCISES: POLITICAL ORIENTATION

Predicting one's political orientation on common, abstractly stated issues is pretty difficult to do. That said, what follows is based on my experience of how an organizer determines another's strategic direction through inference around what he or she is *not*—hardly an ideal measure, but one far easier than predicting what one consciously *is*.

You are less likely to be perceived a "reformer" and be seen as leaning toward other ideological positions if you answer most of the following negatively:

Yes   No

The main problem between groups in society is lack of communication and understanding.

I believe in looking at everyone on their own personal merits, not their occupation or where they live.

Most problems are caused by individuals and the mistakes they make.

"Politics" is just too much talk, especially when there is a problem to solve.

I would work with the devil if it meant we could solve this problem.

You are less likely to be perceived as a social democrat and more likely to be viewed as leaning toward Marxism if you answer the following negatively:

Yes   No

It is possible for capitalism to be reformed if workers are allowed to participate more in decisions that affect the economy.

Society could become socialist without violent upheavel.

Institutions need to be restructured and replaced, not torn down.

It is unfair to think that most trade union leaders have sold out their members.

It is unfair to think that most major civil rights leaders have sold out their communities.

The Democratic party has problems, but if enough good people joined it, it could be transformed into something close to a Labor party.

Chapter 2

KNOW YOURSELF
A Key to Better Organizing

As organizers we often fear we will not be as good as we need to be—
that in fact we are not personally able to do the work well enough (or
are not knowledgeable enough) to perform well. Holding on to this
fear has been the undoing of many organizers, for the simple reality of
organizing life is that good organizers are *always* making mistakes
and being a little less effective than they ought to be. Furthermore,
our slim grass-roots resource base always makes these errors appear
more glaring: You forget to find a meeting place and the leaflet cannot
be done; outreach stops; plans for publicity grind to a halt. People in
larger institutions make the same errors, but no one notices as
quickly, for other tasks can be carried out regardless of the occasional
foul-up. Knowing this helps the grass-roots organizer a little bit, but
just a little. In fact, our slim resource base necessitates some personal
awareness of how we best work, the type of awareness many organizers
too often would prefer ignoring.

While perhaps preferring to ignore personal issues, organizers work
in situations too complex for such a unilaterally cool attitude toward
personal dynamics. The following two examples give some indication
of that complexity.

(1) A few years ago, a young organizer had spent the week working on a
tutorial program proposal—meeting with teachers and students, getting
their ideas, finding out about previous programs' successes and failures.

He had been relatively efficient, and the overall report seemed a good synthesis. A meeting had been called for the potential board of directors to review progress. After a decent introduction, the organizer's response to questions grew more and more irritable. Interaction with others seemed hostile; he seemed to want to "move the agenda," even when the discussion was on the agenda. As time wore on, people were pleased with the outline of his work, but a little perplexed at his method of handling it during the meeting. Likewise, the organizer felt frustrated and drained at the end of the meeting, angry with people's "slowness" but puzzled at why he felt so "antsy" over issues he knew needed to be discussed.

(2) A number of experienced organizers were reviewing their work in the South Bronx over the previous three months. As a group of politically conscious, primarily white activists working in an all Black-Latin neighborhood, they had been trying to develop a political approach to neighborhood revitalization. Some things had gone well—a few people were attending meetings and getting interested in sweat equity programs—but progress were slow. One member was singled out for particular criticism, as his functioning on the street with residents seemed awkward and defensive. The widespread opinion, *including his own,* was that his failure to communicate well on the street was a function of his "poor political understanding of racism." He was expected to read various books and articles and report on his progress at a later date. No attention was ever said to the obvious fact that he was never comfortable in informal settings; all that was sufficient would be for him to learn and change. He never did. Indeed, his tendency toward withdrawn formality seemed to increase.

Both these examples illustrate some important personal questions every organizer needs to answer regarding particular personal strengths and limitations in our work. In the first instance, why was such a nuts-and-bolts meeting so difficult for the organizer to handle? What had really created the defensiveness and irritability? In the second, why did experienced people so easily ignore problems that had little to do with a person's political beliefs? Why did they seek to correct them through a "better political line"? Furthermore, what can be done for any organizer to minimize these problems?

These problems—one common to new organizers, the other to more experienced activists—speak to the heart of the personal side of organizing. Every organizer is quite good in certain areas of work, less effective in others. However, as these two examples suggest, many organizers are unwilling or unable to admit this, not for political reasons, but for personal ones. While we design strategies to be flexible and base our tactical choices on varying levels of available resources, we rarely apply the same standards to *ourselves*, inflexibly and unrealistically expecting ourselves to do whatever needs to be done, even if the results are potentially harmful to the group and, in the long run, taxing to our mental health.

There are two reasons that this happens. One is the often unconscious but nevertheless powerful acceptance of a "great man/woman theory of organizing" that expects us to be all things to all people in all kinds of organizing situations.[1] This is exemplified by Saul Alinsky's criteria for a good organizer in "The Education of An Organizer," which lists everything from political skill to good humor to high levels of intuitive insight as "musts" for your effective work.[2] Such a list is more than a little intimidating, for it leaves the new or inexperienced organizer with a sense of failure, even when her or his skills are quite adequate in many situations. Likewise, experienced organizers come to assume they *should* meet such criteria; if unable to do so, one can "correct" the problem through content-related tasks like reading and political study.

Second, these personality problems are compounded by the basic personality type of most grass-roots organizers. An informal survey of mine conducted over the years has revealed again and again that most organizers (about 70 percent) tend to be much more task- than process-oriented.[3] This means that most organizers prefer outer-directed, content-oriented issues over inner-directed, process-oriented interactions that may involve feelings, emotions, and interpersonal processes rather than mere abstract material. When this content- and outer-directed personal tendency is coupled with the above great man/woman theory of organizing, organizers often foster a blanket attempt to force ourselves through work areas of less personal effectiveness "because we should be able to do them." Indeed, for all our concern with tactics, we often give little thought to the *personal realities of tactical implementation*. "Develop your political perspective, choose your strategy and tactics, and then do it" seems to be a sufficient way to function, saving adroitness for strategic discussion and not one's actual ability to implement desired tactics.

The outcome for these twin issues, as the two painful examples underscore, is that many organizers end up being either less effective or more emotionally drained than they need to be, and thus more likely to leave organizing because of "burnout." Instead of following a few personal guidelines, these activists "push on," even when they are highly irritated with group process, disinterested in fact-finding, uncomfortable with street-smart spontaneity, or whatever. Imagine if you applied these same pressures to others. What kind of an open, democratic organizing approach would that be? It is far more freeing to respect and recognize that you begin this work with certain skills *and* limitations that are heightened or lessened in different organizing situations. You then can learn to use your abilities with greater tactical flexibility. The irony in this kind of humbling self-respect is that it will carry over into greater respect for the people with whom we work, too—by not berating ourselves for limitations that are actually beyond our control, it is less likely we would do the same to others.

There are a number of important procedures to follow in understanding yourself in different situations that can improve tactical effectiveness. (I call this "tactical self-awareness."[4]) First, identify whether or not you are more task-oriented or process-oriented. Don't cop out by saying you are both; everyone should be both, but each of us tends to be more comfortable with one orientation than the other, especially when we are new to this work. I have spent fifteen years of learning how to deal with my task-oriented tendencies, and now can blend process and task *some* of the time, but hardly always. You won't be any different.

Second, review the organizing situations you are involved in and determine whether they emphasize process or task activities. For example, new group situations stress much discussion and group facilitation, which means a process-oriented person will be most effective here. Likewise, specific planning meetings with a high degree of content-focused work and few interpersonal demands means that the situation will be most comfortable for a task-oriented person. Apply this approach to all the activities of the week—street work, meetings, planning sessions, and so on.

Once you go through the situations for their degree of *personal fit* with your own makeup, see if it is possible for you to take greater responsibility for the ones most comfortable for you, getting others to take tasks you find more personally problematic. If this is not possible, build supports for yourself along the way. For example, at longer, process-oriented meetings, I always write a reminder in my organizing notes (or copy of the agenda notice) to "stay calm—people need to talk." This note may seem silly, but it has become a sufficient cue to remind me that the problem in the slow discussion is *with me,* not with others. Likewise, those resistant to fact-finding can allot themselves five specific days in which to do the work instead of the imagined three, allowing for the reality that their tendency to procrastinate will lengthen its completion time. You should provide similar helpful cues in situations that are troublesome for you.

You cannot run away from your limitations, of course, especially in grass-roots organizing, where resources—and personnel—are rarely to be found in abundance. However, when you take on personally more difficult tasks, try not to take on too much at once. You are not too good in informal settings but have to attend that fund-raising party? Try to tend bar or serve food, rather than serving as the official greeter. You dislike office routine but have to help maintain one? Be responsible for keeping the office clean and not keeping the books; whatever mess you make will be quickly visible and easily correctable. Over time you can note improvement and move on to more demanding tasks, but try to start with realistic, modest objectives that are attainable.

Finally, you should consistently work to undermine "great organizer" theories *by judging your progress in personal performance by relative, not absolute, standards.* The group needs to succeed, of course, but here I am talking about your own improvement in the different situations of organizing: from writing to public speaking, from being relaxed in newly formed groups to handling responsibilities for office routine. Real self-respect allows you to be less than perfect, taking pride from improvement that is real improvement for *you,* while perhaps less so for someone else. For example, I am proud that I have an almost-neat and up-to-date filing system. I have known I should have had one for fifteen years; my present filing system has been in place for two. At the same time, I have always worked well in the formation of groups. My desk, unfortunately, is a mess, and I still need to improve daily routines. You should find yourself able to note areas of accomplishment in all parts or organizing, letting progress, however slow, because for quiet satisfaction.

There are other levels where tactical self-awareness is important. Perhaps the two most important relate to (1) often unconsciously derived but quite real difficulties one has with particular individuals, and (2) vestiges of racism, sexism, and class bias that are within all of us.

Tactical self-awareness deals with your awareness of how personally comfortable you are in getting certain tasks done in certain situations. Those situations almost always involve people but at times include certain individuals with whom, for some reason, you do not get along. As grass-roots organizing has few institutional barriers to help minimize interpersonal conflict, it is important to notice when these interpersonal tensions exist for no apparent reason.

For example, I knew someone who always got into arguments with a fellow steering committee member over almost every issue—until she went home to a family picnic and saw the strong physical similarity between her antagonist and a second cousin she disliked. As remarkable as this story is, we all come up against individuals who, for no discernible reason, irritate us. When this happens a little too often and you cannot identify political differences, you find that his or her work is equal to others', and so on, the chances are the problem lies within you. Try to understand its origin, looking over your personal history to identify previous events or individuals who triggered the discomfort.[5]

After you have reflected on this and are sufficiently certain that the problem has little to do with the person's actual behavior, try to get up enough courage to speak with the person about *your* problem. That person will hardly be thrilled by what you have to say (by now you may rub him or her the wrong way, too), but your honesty and willingness to share the personal issue will at least clarify the problem and might lead to a mutually rewarding discussion.

If this fails or you are just not comfortable enough to initiate such an encounter yet, plan in the future to minimize your interactions so that the work is unimpaired. If that is not possible, *work* to lessen your antagonism. For example, make certain you do not comment on their remarks or even raise your hand immediately after he or she has spoken; try not to work on the same subcommittee, especially if they call for a lot of interpersonal interaction.

The other issue, one that infiltrates all organizing, is the unresolved problem of racism, sexism, and class bias lying within us. This topic is too important to leave to the end of one chapter, and it will be discussed later in greater detail. But here it is important to look at the issue in terms of how we can begin undoing problems we want to have but nevertheless find ourselves succumbing to: the sexist joke here, the racist fear or condescending class bias there. Fight as we may to eradicate societal problems, we cannot simply eradicate these feelings by wishing them away. It is far more important—and a lot more effective—to admit they exist and work from there.

In fact, these problems are so universal, *plaguing everyone,* that some of the personal techniques used on racism, sexism, and class bias are quite similar to what has been discussed above. (This realization itself is liberating, for I believe one of the reasons people so rarely admit to these problems is the fear of being singularly identified.) To review, those techniques are:

(1) Identify which areas or issues are most problematic for you. (Don't say "all" and be too guiltily global or "none" and too politically perfect; choose fairly and realistically.)

(2) Once you know them—say, racism and sexism—do not expect to be as effective as you would be under like situations with different people. You won't be.

(3) Bring in supports and other people to make certain the tasks are done well. (I'm not talking about running away from the problem, either, but of realistically dealing with it in the context that other organizing demands need to be met. The only way to un away from these issues in grass-roots organizing is to stop being an organizer.)

(4) Measure your progress in relative, not absolute, terms.

This last is painfully hard to do, for it is hard to admit to racism, sexism, or class bias. No one *should* have any of these problems. But since we do—*and will spend a lifetime in dealing with these issues*—allow yourself to take comfort from the progress you make in confronting your bias, seeing its roots, and learning how to free yourself from that prejudice.[6] It will not be easy, but there is no alternative. Over time, as you relax and learn from others, progress can be made that opens you up to the genuine friendships, trust, and good comradeship that are so much a part of the joys of grass-roots organizing. Just allow yourself time to improve, set out and use techniques to aid in your quest, and the chances are you will achieve your goals with far deeper personal fulfillment and meaning than you ever expected.

This said, let me stress that I am *not* suggesting that relative standards of personal growth as an organizer are a substitute for meeting the absolute needs of people which are the reasons we organizers organize in the first place. At the same time, it is equally important to be less absolute about ourselves and the pace at which we ourselves can change. Indeed, if we can learn to live with and apply these standards where they need to be applied (and not reverse them) <u>our work</u> will undoubtedly be a much richer experience for us all.

NOTES

1. This "theory" and many of the issues discussed here are more fully developed in Steve Burghardt, *The Other Side of Organizing* (Cambridge, MA: Schenkman, 1981), especially Chapters 3 and 4.
2. Saul Alinsky, "The Education of an Organizer," in *Rules for Radicals* (Boston: Beacon Press, 1967).
3. Burghardt, *Other Side,* Chapter 3.
4. See also Steve Burghardt, "Expanding the Use of Self: Steps Toward Tactical Self-Awareness," *Journal of Applied Social Science,* Summer 1981.
5. I am not advocating therapy here, unless one wants to explore these issues in greater emotional depth. One undertakes therapy only if one wants it, not as some prescription to be swallowed whole before one is ready.
6. This is especially hard for people when they first recognize how prevalent racism, sexism, or class bias is. As one organizer put it, "It's horrible. Once I saw how racism works here on the job, I saw it *everywhere*—how people don't look Blacks in the eye, their fears, my hangups, the new TV stereotypes. All I feel is this remorse and anger at myself and everyone else, and I'm feeling like I'll never get off this track—I feel obsessed." This initial "crisis of conscience" phase, if one lets oneself go through it, does pass. You can then go on to use the above techniques effectively. The reason for the first phase's apparently immobilizing power is that it is dealing with material that is objectively obvious and emotionally powerful at the same time. You suffer from "overload" in ways that *do* slow you down. However, this new integration of powerful perceptions and new material is the work to be done here. Accept this, and the process itself will become that much faster.

EXERCISES: TASK VERSUS PROCESS ORIENTATION

Before trying to determine your basic orientation, it is important to begin by identifying certain situations that are either more process- or more task-oriented in their content and demands on the activist.

Higher process-content organizing situations:

●   new group meetings
●   the introductory agenda items at most meetings
●   individual follow-up
●   informal parties and get-togethers

- the "action" part of demonstrations, marches, and so on
- education and communication events, speak-outs, and so on

Higher task-oriented situations
- subcommittee meetings
- controversial, "politically loaded" agenda items
- office routine
- planning meetings
- the running of marches, demonstrations, and so on
- grant writing

Check which of the following task-oriented skills that you are good at:
- running tight-knit meetings
- giving factual reports
- performing subcommittee tasks
- writing
- emphasizing political/economic dynamics in strategy formation
- planning
- organizational maintenance: office routines

Check which of the following process-oriented skills that you are good at:
- running newly formed groups
- preparing social events
- facilitating discussion
- speaking informally
- emphasizing personal/subjective dynamics in strategy formation
- individual follow-up
- organizational maintenance: interpersonal relations

Once you have checked off what you do best and in which situations, look back at a recent meeting in which you were involved. Note the items on the agenda, and divide them into either task- or process-oriented sections. Which items left you feeling most comfortable and most effective? Which ones caused the most problems?

Since any one meeting has other dynamics operating that need to be considered, do this task and process itemization at a few meetings to see what orientation you are personally more comfortable with. Then, as you plan your group's actions over the next month, examine them not only for their political content and strategic considerations but for which of these two orientations seem to dominate, and which items. Try to make assignments accordingly with other members (assuming other considerations are met).

Chapter 3

BUILDING AND MAINTAINING
AN ORGANIZATION

Every organizer needs to understand the structure and processes of groups, their stages of development, and how to work with different types of group members as a group changes and expands.[1] The simplest way to begin thinking about your group and its particular needs is to focus on whether it is new or old. Its age and attendant history (or lack of one) will dictate much about what concerns you and what it is you can do to maximize effectiveness. With this in mind, I shall consider the needs of both newer and older groups and organizer expectations and activities that help fulfill those needs.

NEWER GROUPS

The first and major concern of any organizer working with new, grass-roots groups revolves around whether or not anyone will show up at your first few meetings. Being a decent organizer with normally obsessive qualities, I have *never* slept well before the first meeting of any group I was hoping to get off the ground. This quiet fear in an organizer's stomach, growing larger as we imagine a room full of empty, grey-backed chairs, is the equivalent of stage fright for an actor or actress on opening night; it goes with the turf. The only way a grass-roots organizer can do away with such fears is to stop trying to organize new groups.

The only way to lessen (not stop) these fears is through thorough preparation beforehand. In general, you know who you want to get to the meeting: people from a particular neighborhood, a division of your union local, a group from a hospital's catchment area. Whatever your resources (I assume they are slim), the best rule to follow is that every attempt at systematic outreach should have at least two parts, at least one of which involves *personal* contact—first by flyer or mail, later either by phone or by going to offices, homes, and so on. (Again, this depends on your resources and the size of the group you are trying to form.) If you cannot reach everyone, make a list of "priority" individuals or groups to contact and make certain that at least they know about your new plans. In this way, you increase the likelihood of their interest in you by showing them you are directly interested in them. While this is hardly a guarantee of a packed house, it is the most effective approach you can use to reach new people—one to continue throughout your group's life span (although, of course, you will do so in a more focused way over time, as your membership base becomes established).

Thus, while you will not do away with jitters altogether, carefully targeted outreach will increase the likelihood that people will show up. The next concern, of course, is to keep people coming back to the group after they have shown up once or twice. How can you guarantee that? Unfortunately you cannot and will not. First, do not expect your second meeting, especially in these defensive years, to be as large as the first. You will lose between one-half and one-third the people who attend a first meeting: those who wanted a different type of group, people who saw the group as choosing the wrong issue and are too pessimistic to stick around, the inevitable "crazy" who pushes some bizarre program and leaves forever (you hope). So begin by not expecting more than can be accomplished early on, and communicate that clearly to the group's fellow members. Progressive grass-roots groups can and do grow today. Their growth is slower than we want or hope and will not be as exciting as in times of tremendous momentum. However, if the reasons for this pace are understood, the growth that does occur can give us genuine satisfaction personally and politically.

Indeed, it is important for you and other members in the group to see that success today is measured not only by the attainment of group objectives (which may take a long time to accomplish and are abstractly distant at first) but by *whether or not you are expanding the activist core.* The easiest way to calm your nerves over whether or not the group will be successful is by knowing that this expansion is occurring.

All grass-roots groups seem to have three important membership layers: the activists, the helpers, and the communicators.[2] The *activists* are those willing to take primary responsibility for how the group functions. They will help put out the newsletter, coordinate the outreach work, and so on. Few people will *begin* at this level, for this means real work. You can assume that the movement of people to this level of activity is a sign of commitment, a sign concrete enough to let you know, even before campaigns are finished and objectives are met, that the group has staying power.

The *helpers* are people who will not take consistent responsibility for the group, but will function on a consistent but limited basis. For example, helpers will not help prepare a newsletter, but they will distribute it once a month in their building, worksite, or neighborhood. Furthermore, they are invaluable as barometers of how the group is being perceived by others, for their commitment is high enough to care about the group but low enough not to be blinded to others' criticisms or concerns (which does happen to activists at times). Over time, many such helpers do move into the activist ranks, especially if the group appears successful.

The *comunicators* do not perform functional tasks for the group, but they are aware of its presence and are willing to discuss its issues, occasionally attend meetings of interest, and, at times, attend rallies and demonstrations that seem important to them. Their lack of overall commitment to the group means that particular individuals may be erratic in what they communicate about the group and what it is doing; collectively, however, such people tell you if you are being received well and if your campaigns are picking up momentum through expanded interest and involvement.

Remember, all three types of members are important to any grassroots group, each serving different functions and fulfilling particular needs. As stated earlier, however, the expansion of the activist core, by its concreteness, is the easiest and earliest measure of a new group's potential success. The bonus here is that it can help calm an organizer's jittery nerves. (Don't forget that the newness to a group means that much of its time will be spent on education, communication, and process-oriented work—just the kind of activities that most oranizers wish to complete quickly.)

THE THREE MAIN TASKS FOR A NEW GROUP

There are three complementary tasks of which an organizer to be aware during a new group's development: the manner and substance of general meetings, follow-up with and involvement of potential members, and the substantive work of task-oriented subcommittees. First, the organizer makes certain that new group meetings allow for good, consistent communications by as many people as possible concerning the issue or issues that brought them together. This means that the group activists (including the organizer) need to be prepared on what the group is about and yet be willing to let others speak on whatever concerns them. Speakers should be informative and moderately brief. Note that I said "moderately," not just "brief." People want information first, not a quick, overly modest run-through followed by complete openness—that is a false form of democratic decision making. Democracy assumes knowledge, which means people need and want information in order to be decision makers. Otherwise there would be no need for the group in the first place. The best mix is clear, concise information (the outline of which should be included on an introductory, 200-word flyer, if possible) coupled with a chance for speaking out and dialogue. Finally, specific action-oriented reports, which give the group a semblance of life, should be presented and should emphasize concrete information, not boring details. Once explained, see if there are volunteers to sign up for work on these actions, and have a sign-up sheet available for them to do so![3]

Meetings that are open, flexible, and concrete in their actions are only one part of an organizer's task with a new group. Equally important is what goes on after general meetings are held. First, you and the other activists should ascertain who seemed most interested in the group. (Include here "good listeners" as well as "good talkers." Many people who don't publicly volunteer for a subcommittee may just be hesitant to do so in front of large groups.) Make certain your meeting sigh-up sheets include space for a home address and phone numbers (activists should sign first to serve as an example for others to follow—printing clearly, including zip codes, and so on).[4]

This targeted list become the focus of the activist's second set of tasks. The importance of follow-up visits or phone calls during a new group's life cannot be underestimated. Most people are not used to others actually paying attention to them. By doing so after a meeting or two, you begin to communicate volumes about the democratic nature of your group. The conversation should be centered on the group's specific tasks (as seen through the meeting's committee reports and the "general discussion" topic) *but discussed in the potential activist's terms*—as he or she sees things, not necessarily as you do. Find out what new members liked and disliked, which work seemed most interesting and why. Listen to their manner of speaking—what excites them and what doesn't—as much as to what they say. Furthermore, don't just pump them for information but share some of your own ideas and feelings about the meetings; otherwise, they are the only ones risking anything in the conversation. Above all, be honest: Admit mistakes, state disagreements fairly, and add information that clears up confused perceptions.

Finally, make certain to invite new members to subcommittee meetings held between the last general meeting and the next one. See if they need transportation or child care. Give them your name and phone number and that of one other person on the subcommittee. (One of you should call a night or two before the subcommittee meeting to remind them of the meetings, where it is being held, and similar details.)

The subcommittee itself, while still somewhat informal, should be focused on specific tasks. It should be held a week—no more than two—after the general meeting to show the group's forward momentum. It concentrates on specific *objectives* (say the preparation of a newsletter) that will be concretely discussed in terms of specific task-oriented actions (writing articles, getting certain people to write, planning distribution). Where the general meeting is more open-ended and concerned with discussion of *goals* (which can be vague), the subcommittees are directed more toward the completion of concrete objectives designed to help achieve those goals.

All of this work shows the new members and potential activists an alive, involved group that is doing things of which they can be part. The larger meetings are used to share information and hear concerns, which suggests democratic participation and knowledge building; the individual follow-up demonstrates openness and individualized concern; the concrete work of the subcommittee suggests an energetic group trying to improve things. Together, this blend of process-oriented activities, follow-up, and concrete action (all spread out in manageable chunks of time) create the likelihood of a group surviving in the 1980s (assuming the issue is important *and* there are enough resources to struggle along).

OLDER GROUPS

Older groups and their organizers face a different set of concerns from those of new groups. Indeed, many organizers become bored with well-established groups, viewing their maintenance as a sign of stagnation rather than success. This concern is often unjustified; it speaks more to why organizers personally seem to prefer action and change to stability and stasis. It is important that you apply tactical self-awareness in such stabilized situations before prematurely assuming the group has "sold out."

Not that the concern is never without justification; indeed, there is often enough truth in one's fears to warrant at least their perpetuation. The most common problems facing established[5] grass-roots groups (beyond the political threat of cooptation that some groups may or may not face, depending on ideology) are (1) a self-satisfied inwardness, which over time breeds marginality and a lack of outward growth, and (2) a tendency toward undemocratic and elitist functioning.

The easiest way to identify the early signs of inwardness is the tendency for group members to begin talking in "alphabet soup," or shorthand: "The CDRs visited the main office the other evening, and John spoke really well on the 'anti' issue" is an example—a real one that a student told me. The statement left her and every other new individual in the room shaking their heads in bewilderment. As you can see, besides alphabet soup, this tendency includes first names (John) and short-hand words ("anti") that communicate only to those-in-the-know. It is a symptom of a group that looks *only* to its own members for guidance and feedback. Outreach cannot really exist, for new people cannot be expected to comment on such vague and obscure subjects, let alone feel comfortable discussing issues in unfamiliar terms.

Of course, it is inevitable that old-timers will begin to use some short-hand. Organizers and other long-term group activists must first serve as role models by minimizing their tendency to alphabetize. Second, they must carefully but consistently intervene when "alphabetizers" speak, so that unfamiliar, terms are clarified quickly. Written agendas and flyers should never have abbreviations on them (unless a name is well known and/or the group seeks to be identified by its acronym. Discussion of new-member issues and education must be alloted a specific (and preferably early) slot on the agenda so that new people can understand what is going on as much as possible.

Outreach in the way it was earlier described must be carried on through the life of an organization. While, understandably, it will be more focused due to other group needs, you must establish from the beginning a group norm of searching for and respecting new members' needs, interests, and perceptions. Once dropped, it is very difficult to reestablish. The other, more concrete work seems more important and exciting. If treated as being as integral to your group's survival as, say, fund-raising, this ongoing outreach keeps your group alive to new and potentially invaluable members who otherwise would be lost. In the process, this norm of outward, searching activity helps balance older-member tendencies of inward, high-powered, focused energy.

Finally, subcommittee work, even though its ongoing, concrete focus may make it appear repetitive to you and other old-timers, is brand new and potentially confusing to new people. If new people are in the room, subcommittee reports at general meetings should always briefly give information on why it was formed. "Alphabetitis" should especially be avoided here, for the subcommittee's concrete work is the best example to newcomers of what the group is about—or it can be the easiest material to be turned off to.

This emphasis on procedural items for explanation, clarity in communication, and clear terminology may seem to be overly concerned with process, but I believe it is not. In the establishment of these democratic norms—norms that speak of respect for new, "uninformed" people—you establish how deep a commitment your older group has to genuine democratic change and growth from the outside. Every group expresses its desire for newcomers, of course, but it is easy enough to see if such sentiments are actually practiced. If they are not, the group will not grow.

Older members also have needs that must be met by the newly established group. First, there is the need to feel one's work is worthwhile. The subcommittees should help serve this function, but general meetings should always allow for concrete reports that publicly validate the efforts of various members. Here I am not talking about falsely praising people to keep them involved, but rather giving genuine, public respect to people who work hard for a group. Too often, in our task-oriented haste to get on with our work, attention to such small detail may seem minor, but it is a small contribution to the overall democratic functioning of a group.

Second, make certain that part of your group's activities contain some form of political education and development. The type of politics depends on the group's ideological concerns, but its purpose is consistent in every group: to keep group members aware of larger group goals, concerns, and issues, so that their own tasks are not magnified out of proportion and their group continues to deepen and widen its core of *skilled* activists. Established groups always run the risk that their dedicated members will begin to see their subcommittee tasks as more important than those of the group itself. Anyone who works many hours a week on some project is bound to feel this way somewhat; ongoing study, training sessions, and the like help keep people oriented toward broader topics of greater importance than their own work. As long as that work is validated in consistent ways somewhere else (as mentioned above), the members can become increasingly sophisticated in their ability to perform—and be appreciative of— almost all functions of the group's life.

The final issue for established groups—one that must be dealt with early in its life—will be the nature of leadership.[6] You must begin with whatever people assume is necessary (to do otherwise is to court disinterest), but a general principle to work toward is *the greater the shared decision making, the greater the long-term benefits for membership and group alike.* Do not forget, in a conservative and, for us, defensive period like this one, that there is a real need to concentrate on developing as many people as possible for important responsibilities in the future. To have a small grass-roots group dominated by one or two people is not worth much when it could be serving as a training ground for twenty highly skilled activists in the future. The bulk of this chapter, from "alphabet soup" to "outreach discussion in their terms," has been based on this principle of sharing decision making as widely as possible for what it can help develop for tomorrow.

Most of these issues have been procedural in nature. I can also suggest two structural issues to work toward. First, the group should limit a person's position as head of the organization to no more than two years. I am not saying the group should deny people leadership (it just resurfaces in new, disguised forms) but that the health of a group necessitates some consistent turnover in high-level responsibility and decision making if it is to survive as a democratic group. If ongoing training, shared decision making, and respect for democratic norms has been maintained, this need not be a problem. Talented people will be there to replace other talented people, who in turn remain available and active in the group in ways that can be revitalizing to the group—taking over responsibility for a less-than-effective subcommittee, for example.

Second, no one in the group should be excused from performing all the tasks involved in grass-roots group life. The tendency toward a division of labor so permeates our lives that it is quite easy to assume, like most institutions, that experienced, leading members of our groups do not need to perform "menial" tasks (giving out flyers, cleaning the office, typing). While new members will do more of this because of their inexperience and their need to learn the ropes of how the group functions, older members cannot use their status as a vehicle to exclude themselves from the tasks that are repetitive and physically tiring to do. Indeed, such work is usually a key to a group's continued growth and expansion, since it forces experienced members to maintain contact with both a layer of the membership and the group's constituency that they too often lose. Furthermore, the performance of these tasks once again speaks decisively about the true democratic nature of the group.[7]

CONCLUSION

While there are degrees of difference bred by experience and varying membership needs, the actual functions of the older and newer groups are not different. Each must have good, open general meetings, outreach, and focused subcommittees. The newer group balances the fear of failure with the excitement of its energy and potential; the older balances its established success with the danger of inwardness and undemocratic functioning. The organizer's task is to work to minimize the potential problems of each. With new groups, he or she works to avoid failure *through careful planning around short-term tasks* that can achieve success and boost momentum. For older groups, he or she tries to avoid its dangers *through planning and maintaining long-term process issues* that emphasize outward-looking democratic values, regardless of the concrete tasks before the membership.

By looking at how groups work, it becomes clear, as Rothman, Freire, and others have noted, that process and task can never be fully separated.[8] A good group whether old or new, if it has a decent issue and a modicum of resources, will only succeed in the long run because its members understood this from its inception.

NOTES

1. See, for example, Margaret Hartford, *Social Work with Groups* (New York: Columbia University Press, 1974); Steve Burghardt, "Group Dynamics as Dialectical Practice," in *The Other Side of Organizing* (Cambridge, MA: Schenkman, 1982), and "A.C.O. Typology of Group Development," in Cox et al., *Strategies of Community Organization* (Itasca, IL: Peacock, 1978).

2. *All* types are important to the group, and all should be respected for the level of activity they choose to play. Remember, it is far better to get someone who over time becomes a committed activist than it is to force activism on someone who quits the group—and all grass-roots work—in three months.

3. A discussion on how to run meetings will be covered in the next chapter.

4. Be careful to write "phone number (if any)," as many poor people cannot afford the luxury of their own phone. The "if any" communicates your respectful awareness of this small but hardly trivial reality of many poor people's lives.

5. "Established" is a tricky word for a grass-roots group. Here I mean a group that has its own resource base and is recognized by others as a legitimate force in the community involved in the issue, in the union, in its reference group, and so on—that is, a group whose actions and ideas must be taken seriously.

6. A more theoretical discussion of this issue takes place in Burghardt, "Leadership Development: Moving from 'Helping' to 'Sharing,' " *Social Development Issues,* 1981/1982, Vol. 5, Nos. 1 and 2.

7. Jack Rothman, "Three Models of Community Organization Practice," in Cox et al., *Strategies,* pp. 20-37; Paulo Freire, *Pedagogy of the Oppressed* (New York: Seabury Press, 1972), pp. 44-49.

8. Steve Burghardt, "Contradictions of Leadership Development for the 1980's," paper delivered at the National Symposium of Community Organization and Planning, Louisville, Kentucky, March 1981.

EXERCISES: INCREASING INVOLVEMENT

If you want to increase involvement, your group must have activities available that reflect the different stages of involvement of your membership. Do you have them in place? Or do they all tip in only one direction?

for communicators: 1. monthly meetings
                        2. educational sessions
                        3. coalition-type efforts with other groups
for helpers: 4. letter writing
                        5. leafletting

for activists:	6. newsletter distribution
	7. subcommittee work and leadership
	8. steering committee work and planning
	9. grant and proposal preparation

In analyzing meetings, begin by noting the number of activists, helpers, and communicators. What was the balance among the three groups? Did anyone new seem to move into the activist circle? Our of it? What attempts were made to help people become more active? To support them for the level of involvement they were at?

Activists need action and involvement; communicators need information; and helpers are somewhere between. Did your meeting agenda reflect these varying needs and interests? Were sign-up lists available before and during the meeting? Were follow-up arrangements made? How long did they take to be made?

Not every event will have equal numbers of activists, helpers, and communicators. The following inventory of different actions can give you an idea of what to expect and how to rate your successful growth as a multilayered, involved group.

1. subcommittee meetings: high in activists only
2. general meetings: equal mix of activists and helpers, with some communicators
3. leafletters: more helpers than activists (through activists may work longer hours)

4. forums and educationals: higher in helpers, activists, and com-
munitators than at other events, with some decent numbers of new,
uncategorized people

5. demonstrations: high in all three groups, with new people, communicators, and helpers outnumbering activists

Chapter 4

PLANNING AND RUNNING MEETINGS

Meetings are the essence of a grass-roots group's life. That essence is hardly pure or sweetly distilled, but without them grass-roots organizations could not function. Our resources are people and people-based actions, so meetings must be held—often. It's a shame so many of them are so horrible to sit through.

Meetings don't have to be horrible, but running a good meeting in an open, democratic, firm way is a very difficult skill to master. A chairperson needs to be familiar with the people in attendance, have a good grasp of the issues so that he or she can synthesize and clarify, and be strong when people become unruly and yet flexible when people have a need to know. It's no wonder that most new organizers worry about their skills in chairing a meeting. After the concern about getting people to a meeting, concerns over not making a meeting a mess seem to rank second in the beating hearts of new organizers.

Before turning to how one runs actual meetings, there are a few other issues to discuss. *First, the meeting actually begins with its flyer or announcement.* Keep the flyer simple, easy to read, with pertinent information (including time, place, date, and a "for more information" name, phone number, and address), and prominently displayed. If you wish to analyze some issue or describe your group, do

AUTHOR'S NOTE: *For a good, more traditionally focused approach to the funding of meetings, see John Tropman,* Effective Meetings: Improving Group Decision-Making *(Beverly Hills, CA: Sage, 1980).*

so, briefly, on the other side of the flyer. (If you cannot afford that, put all the pertinent factual material at the top, and place your analysis at the bottom in a separate box.[1] Most people will spend between ten and fifteen seconds looking at a flyer; if it catches their interest, they read on. A neat, attractive flyer is a good beginning for your meeting; it increases the likelihood of a good turnout.

General meetings should start within fifteen minutes of their publicized time, and no exceptions should be made, especially when the group is new. It is easy to establish a reputation of either promptness or sloppiness, and equally hard to break it. It is unfair to those who are on time to wait for others less concerned with or indifferent to efficient meetings. You can always schedule nonessential but appropriate items at the beginning of the meeting to allow others ample time to hear the most substantive part of the meeting. But don't capitulate to tardiness by starting later and later—it's a dead end.

General meetings should not run more than two to two and a half hours—three at the most. (Subcommittee meetings, where substantive work by activists goes on, may be longer.) If you are serious about attracting poor and working-class people to your group, you will hold to this time limit, for they have to get up early for work (as do parents of young children). Furthermore, people can process only so much material at one time. If you do go beyond three hours, the group will be overloading its membership in a way that makes democratic decision making impossible. People may vote, but often will do so from a desire to end the meeting rather than on substantive grounds. Such decision making—and the time-wasting content that creates it—can hardly aid a group in the long run.

Try to provide child care. Small groups with limited space are often strapped to provide child care, but women and working parents in general must have child care available if they are to be ongoing, active members of the group. The only guarantee to new members that this issue is treated seriously is that a group provides child care from its inception, rotating *all* men and women in the organization in its maintenance. Just because men are initially uncomfortable with child care is no excuse for their avoiding the task. Indeed, it is one of the few ways other than parenting we have to learn how to nurture, and should be appreciated accordingly. Men must be involved consistently in child care, no matter how "correctly" some may complain about their potential mishandling of kids. Kids can handle two hours even with a klutz, and probably can teach him a lot in the process!

Prove your credentials on class, race, and sex early on. If your meeting is run only by white males—or by a token individual here or there—it is impossible to maintain your credibility for long. At the same time, oppressed people in general are not as active as others, all rhetoric aside, and people should not falsely accuse grass-roots groups of failing to achieve widespread racial, sexual, and cross-occupational harmony and joint activity when no one else has either. Therefore, do not put people in spotlights when they are ill-prepared for major public roles. By providing realistic, concrete, and relevant tasks for a range of your membership to participate in publicly, you clearly communicate that your group places value in *seeking to build* a heterogeneous, nonbiased organization. Such a reputation is hard to get, but, if there are negative reviews on early performances, harder still to change. Be conscious of this early on and you stand a chance of establishing a reputation you can be proud of.

RUNNING A GRASS-ROOTS MEETING

There are four organizational factors to consider in planning your meeting: (1) the size of the group, (2) the percentage of new people attending, (3) the social mix of the group, and (4) the degree and intensity of difference among attendees' competing reference groups. (In general, the more any of these factors will be operating at your meeting, the more careful planning you will need. If you are holding a meeting with large, new, heterogeneous, and competing groups of attendees, you are holding some kind of political convention, so hire a parliamentarian and hope that there's a blizzard the night before!)

Actually, general meetings for grass-roots fall into two general categories: (1) meetings that because of their large size and/or newness of attendees demand planning that emphasizes *thematic orchestration;* (2) meetings that because of their social mix and/or potentially competing reference groups demand planning that emphasizes *firm but democratic procedures.*

If you wish to emphasize thematic orchestration, plan to "show off" the group in a series of reports and discussions that explain the nature of the group, its pertinent issues, and how others can become involved with you. A more open process of give and take underscores the themes you are developing through scheduled time for open discussion and questions. The agenda should begin with a brief introduction by the chairperson, who explains the group and why the meeting is being held. If there are fewer than twenty people, you may want everyone to introduce themselves and where they are from; if more than twenty, ask people to give the same information when they speak. However, do not let people present more in their introductions; name and place is enough. The rest can, and will, come out through discussion.

The initial agenda items should be two or three action-oriented, concrete reports by a number of members, showing the group's diversity and activity. You want to show people that the group is active and alive. If done early on, these reports can stimulate their interest. These reports also help orient people to the group. Do not forget that what is familiar to you may be murky for others, and these reports can bring into concrete focus the nature of the group before people are expected and needed to participate at a greater level in the meeting.

The next agenda item should relate to the central purpose for the meeting. The first items have developed the themes of your activism and have helped clarify general issues. This item is the one that has brought these new (and, with luck, many) people together where the activity's purpose is deepened through some analysis, discussion, and presentation that will motivate people to become more involved in the group. If you assume that the first three reports took around fifteen minutes, plan on thirty minutes for the presentation and the same amount of time for feedback and discussion. The chairperson's task here (assuming the presentation itself does not ramble on) is to make certain he or she calls on a wide variety of people, facilitating discussion by synthesizing various comments so the audience understands everything, and moving discussion to new topics as others grow repitipive or seem finished.

Here the chair and other activists need to know as much as possible about the themes of the group and its most pertinent issues, using analytic skills for clarifying and synthesizing so that the group discussion moves along smoothly. It is less important that the chair be a skilled parliamentarian, as nice as that might be. Thematic clarity, a knowledge of group issues, and enthusiasm for what the group is trying to do are most important.

The discussion should be followed up with concrete tasks or subcommittees for which people can volunteer, and sign-up sheets should be passed around (give it to a willing activist first to provide momentum and to fill out the sheet correctly). Final announcements, time, date and place of the next meeting, and the like should be made quickly, and, if you can afford it, refreshments should be provided during the follow-up work. Don't be afraid to pass the hat, preferably right after the discussion is over (and before people have left).

RUNNING HETEROGENEOUS AND/OR POTENTIALLY CONFLICTUAL MEETINGS

The above meetings demand planning and create nervousness at times, but the emphasis on thematic clarity makes the events relatively placid. They can be equally calm when you have a wide social mix of races, sexes, and classes, especially if the groups have had a common work or community experience that unites them in common cause. If that exists, much of the discussion below is not necessary; one should use the previous discussion as one's guide. Unfortunately, one of the sad realities of the early 1980s is that there are few lasting heterogeneous coalition organizations in our midst. There still is not enough trust between races, sexes, and people of different sexual preferences and occupations to enable these different social groups to work together comfortably. Thus, while not wanting a new grass-roots initiative to fail, people do not expect a new group to work for them, either, and therefore they are sensitive to potentially exclusionary procedures and may perceive indifference to their being heard in equal measure with all others in the group.

Likewise, we cannot forget that grass-roots groups usually spring up at least in part out of disagreement with the way some part of their community (or a large institution) is being run. This means they are operating in a field where conflict is as common as crabgrass. There will be people, often well organized and highly skilled, who would like nothing more than to see your group fall apart. Potential conflict is a grass-roots reality that no organizer can afford to ignore.

When these issues dominate your meetings (or, as sometimes happens, when they arrive hand-in-hand), your group can minimize problems by knowing how to run a firm, strong meeting that gets its business done—and does so without sacrificing democratic principles in the process.[2]

Here the key lies in the group activists having a decent, workable understanding of Robert's Rules of Order. I know that some people will sneer at these techniques, feeling they are too artificial and top-heavy for a grass-roots group to use. They may be right—Robert's Rules aren't as pleasant and relaxed as just talking and taking voice votes—but the alternatives, especially in conflict situations, are much worse. For example, "consensus" voting, where people discuss an issue until a formulation is reached with which everyone agrees, is in my experience both elitist and undemocratic. It is elitist because consensus meetings can go on for hours—hours that working people and parents do not have. It is undemocratic because it assumes that disagreement is a sign of group weakness rather than actual strength. To my mind, there is nothing more democratic than a group that fights out an issue and, once votes are taken, finds all its members working to implement the majority decision. The "losers" in the debate have not had to sacrifice their beliefs; the group has not had to sacrifice its activity. Consensus politics usually sacrifices both.

Another meeting format that is not very helpful occurs when activists, wanting to appear "nice," allow discussion to wander without resolution. Not wanting to test the clear waters of democratic decision making for fear of alienating some potential activist (who may have different social characteristics from most group members), the group leaders avoid ever specifically finalizing an action on strategy in yes or no terms. This means that responsibility for decision making will rest only with those involved in implementing group actions, that is, the leadership itself. Members, by never taking votes on clearly delineated issues, thus lose their control over how their leaders implement policy—hardly a model of organization we need to foster today.

For all its ills, I have found that a *modified* form of Robert's Rules of Order, agreed upon by the membership early in the group's history and simple enough to explain quickly in the midst of a meeting, works best.[3] While a group must adapt and develop the set of procedures it deems best, the most important are those that can maintain a semblance of order without sacrificing democratic functioning. Those are (1) making and seconding motions, (2) calling or moving the "question" (voting to end the discussion on a particular motion), (3) making amendments, and (4) making procedural motions for membership clarification. I know there are others of value—especially those related to the role of chairperson—but most grass-roots groups do not need more than this, even when conflict is intense. (Remember, if you become too rule-oriented and procedural you will drive off many good people who are either intimidated or bored by the unsubstantial hoopla.)

When there is an important and conflictual issue before your group, it is best for the chairperson to ask for a motion early on so that the group has something concrete on which to focus. By having a motion made and seconded,[4] the group can argue its points more clearly. Other motions (about implementation, for example) can be politiely but firmly ruled "out of order," so that the main discussion is well rounded and complete.

The person making the motion must do so without speaking on the motion itself at the same time. This limits bias in the discussion, although it is common practice to let the maker of the motion speak at some point. Likewise, most grass-roots groups do not mind the chair speaking as long as the person is fair in the rest of her or his functioning. If you call on an equal number of people representing the different positions in the room, no one can accuse you of being heavy-handed.

Once discussion has gone on long enough for some clarity, someone from the floor (therefore *not* the chair) may raise her or his hand and, *if called upon,* "move the question" (again without comment on the motion). (There are technical differences between "moving" and "calling" the question, but most grass-roots groups ignore them.) Once a motion to "move the question" (to end discussion) has been made and seconded, all discussion on the main motion stops. It is the chair's responsibility to advise the group that they are *voting on whether or not to end discussion in order to vote on the main motion, not that they are voting yes or no on the main motion.* Hands are raised and votes taken. If a majority votes no, discussion continues. If yes, the chair then asks either the recording secretary or (more likely) the maker of the motion to read back the *original motion only.* (He or she has no right to embellish at this point.) The vote is then taken, and if it is no, the agenda is moved to a new item or new motions are offered on the same issue. If it is yes, the problem of implementation—who will do what and when—is either handled then by the group or, if the group agrees, referred to the appropriate committee.

Amendments usually serve two distinct purposes. If the discussion is intense enough that there appear to be a number of ways to handle an issue, then group members have the right to offer other positions via amendments. An amendment is made exactly as a motion is, and often serves certain tactical purposes either of clarification or of counterposing two alternative positions through the amendment and the main motion. (For example, the amendment may say "do not endorse a strategy against cooperative housing," while the main motion says "do endorse an anticooperative apartment strategy.") Once made, that amendment is what is to be discussed. When votes are taken, people are to vote on the last amendment first, proceeding to vote on the main motion last.

Amendments also serve to distinguish between perceived good and bad parts of the main motion. (For example, an amendment may oppose cooperative housing in apartments with six or more units, while the main motion opposes all cooperative housing.) This can be a procedural trap to confuse people if too many amendments are made, and a good chair will work to limit their number and their complexity. This takes real skill, but outside of major conventions or conferences, a grass-roots group should rarely have to become too procedurally technical in its debates. Formulated correctly, these amendments can clarify and satisfy the group, so *all* members should learn how to make them.

This is especially true in the use of other "procedural" requests and motions. Used too often, they are undemocratic; used correctly, they can help a chair restore order and maintain movement on an important debate. The technique most commonly used is to say "point of procedure" and thus be immediately called upon by the chair. "Point of procedure" receives priority over the main discussion because the caller is *requesting information*—asking if the topic is being kept to, how much time is left in the debate, and so forth. However, the person calling point of procedure can only ask a short question; embellishing it with intense feelings (no matter how strong they are) is not allowable, and a chair must quickly rule any further comments "out of order" (while answering the procedural question).

All of these procedural points can be amplified, and each has enough exceptions to warrant a host of explanatory footnotes. My intention here is only to present the basics on how to run a fair but firm meeting. Differences based on group needs, experience, cultural expectations, and so forth can and will be dealt with by you. It is clear, however, that whatever the nature of your group and the demands of a particular meeting, there must be a good working relationship between the chair and other group members. The chair must be experienced, especially in tense meetings; anything else is unfair to everyone and will probably result in a disaster.[5] But members, knowing that every meeting requires widespread, focused participation, need to know to responsibly make motions, introduce speakers, and the like. Today it is inevitable that we will often disagree on the nature of our work and the best course to follow in building a solid grass-roots movement. It is not inevitable that we can do so either easily or democratically—even though we must if we are to succeed. The best option for minimizing poor functioning that later slides into overly undemocratic methods and ineffective shortcuts is to learn these procedures, plan on *working* to maintain democracy, and labor to make our groups models for the types of organizations we need in the future. After all, there is nothing wrong with debate; done well, it enhances whatever we seek to become. As the past has taught us all too clearly, there are no substitutes.

NOTES

1. For an inexpensive but attractive way to make your flyer, buy some "press type" from a local stationery or art supply store. Use the bolder letters for the main announcement and pertinent information like time and place. Longer, descriptive material can be typed. Use only black ink; blue tends to photocopy poorly.

2. Don't forget that meeting planning sessions should educate all members to what may lie ahead at the meeting.

3. A very good phamplet on Robert's Rules of Order is available through your local League of Women Voters. It is short, clear, and helpful. One issue it does not cover is who has voting rights. Each group decides this for itself, but it is important to establish some precedent that voting is based on previous attendance and/or activity. This avoids any danger of someone packing your meetings too easily.

4. Having a "second" to a motion may seem like a waste of time until you have one obnoxious or poorly focused individual with little support at a meeting. The way to quiet such a person—fairly—is to ask her to him for a motion and then request a second. Without one, the troublemaker's issue dies (at least for that meeting). From that point on the chair can rule discussion on the issue "out of order" without being undemocratic.

5. The best way to practice being a chairperson is in small subcommittees and by being an effective person procedurally in the meetings, making motions, adding clarifying amendments and participating in other ways.

EXERCISES: PLANNING MEETINGS

1. Review recent past meetings that worked well and others that did not. Note breakdowns that occurred, and why. Were the problems caused by poor planning or would preparation not have mattered? (For example, "crazies" or disrupters are always hard to deal with.) If a similar meeting with the same basic membership/audience is planned in the future, what specific corrections are you going to make?

2. Is the next meeting well planned? What are the objectives—that is, what does your group hope to accomplish by the time the meeting is over?
   a. Does your agenda reflect the needs and composition of your audience?
   b. How skillful a chairperson do you need?
   c. Are handouts available on complicated but important matters that need discussion?
   d. Have you contacted speakers regarding their topics and considered how each relates to your objectives?
   e. Have important contacts, potential activists, and others been personally reached before the meeting?
   f. Are sign-up sheets ready?
   g. Are people taking care of refreshments?
   h. Are those responsible for child care committed to doing it well?
   i. Will someone be making a fund-raising or contributions pitch?
   j. Has a clean-up committee been formed?

---

3. On your functioning:
   a. Do you help greet people and make them feel more comfortable, or is this kind of task uncomfortable for you?
   b. Do you help tidy the place up, run the literature table, and the like?
   c. Do you tend to stand around and talk with old-timers only?
   d. What type of speaking role do you like to take? Do you emphasize content, or do you tend to facilitate others' points when you talk?
   e. Do you make it a point to speak with new people after the meeting?
   f. Do you ever *volunteer* for clean-up, child care, refreshments, and other work, or do you try to avoid such tasks as much as possible?

Chapter 5

MAINTAINING DAILY ROUTINES

Almost nothing has been written about the daily routines followed by grass-roots organizations. Perhaps this is because people assume there are no routines, just erratic, ad hoc decisions that are carried out pell-mell as the need arises. Unfortunately, anyone who takes such an ad hoc approach dooms their group before it ever has a chance to grow, especially during the tight times of the early 1980s.

Organizers who are good at running meetings and developing actions are rarely the best people for maintaining good day-to-day functioning for their group. A quieter, more "laid-back," punctual person is best for handling the main responsibilities here. At the same time, do not expect *anyone* to be as efficient as equivalent people in large-scale organizations. Our resource base is too constricted, our economies of scale too small to allow for the greater efficiency of large-scale organizations.[1] They'll be good, but our expectations on what is and isn't efficient has to fit the size of our group and the energy, commitment, and resources available for it.

What usually seems to bother new organizers about daily routines is that there seems to be so much to do, and most of it is all over the place, scattered and unfocused. Being task-oriented, we find that this large amount of scattered minutiae create in us a desire to "do it all"—make the phone calls, do the follow-up, plan the flyer, rent the hall, and so on. We then confuse our own discomfort in having so little immediate control over this situation with a distrust of other people's abilities to perform what are essentially simple tasks—tasks that are nevertheless the heartbeat of the organization. In fact, in being shared by as wide a spectrum of the membership as possible, these tasks both train people in skills for the future and socialize everyone in the concrete experience of taking control over how we live at least part of our lives. In short, the performance of daily tasks carries with it the essence of self-determination. It is therefore of no small importance that we learn how to structure our routines democratically—and thus put a check on our often unconscious tendencies to try to control too much of this work.

Two basic principles underlie the successful maintenance of day-to-day routines. First, the only sure way that people will feel confident about the tasks of policy implementation—and that's what daily routines are—is for there to have been thorough political discussion by the membership on what the tasks and objectives of the group are. Such collective decision making creates confidence that the individuals responsible for carrying out group wishes will understand what they are, and are not, to do. Lacking that kind of decision making, group members are much more open to charges of misdirection or mishandling of group tasks by other members. If you wish to begin feeling comfortable about what you and others are to do day to day, have well-worked out group decisions to serve as a guide. This is especially true as the group expands and newcomers, understandably not familiar with how things are done, look for justifications of the way things function. If plans of implementation have been formally agreed upon in the past, they will be a lot easier for others to accept in the future.

Second, *everyone,* regardless of his or her official position or length of experience, should be expected to participate in the mundane as well as the dramatic events of grass-roots organizational life. Everyone should be expected at some time to do mailings, make phone calls, or clean an office. Leaving it up to only the newcomers suggests that such work is irrelevant rather than vital to group maintenance and growth. This is especially true if your group wishes to break down some of the assumptions about class and social status. While leaders will need to be involved in more directly political strategy sessions in ways that newcomers cannot completely understand, to relegate only new members to the "busy work" means they will never completely understand. That can do little for your desire for a truly democratic group.

With these two political principles helping orient your daily work, day-to-day routines become smoother and less personally troublesome for task-oriented activists. The tasks themselves should be delegated to the appropriate subcommittees, or, if there are none, to the overall coordinating or steering committee. When the tasks are to be done collectively—here that means anything involving more than one person—try to create a social atmosphere around the work itself. Plan to have dinner together, have some wine or beer, or listen to music. When the tasks have a lot of time but are not exactly stimulating in their complexity, this social atmosphere goes a long way in maintaining *esprit de corps,* especially today. Furthermore, it is a chance for you and others informally to discuss political/organizational issues on a wide range of topics, getting to know each other in the process.

Each committee should set up objectives for the month (or week, depending on how often it meets). Those objectives should be concrete, with expected completion dates and the name of each person responsible written down in the committee chairperson's notebook. A telephone tree should be set up, through either the coordinating committee or the various subcommittees. Each member gets the numbers of a few people to call, who in turn call others until the entire membership has been reached. By assigning names to each subcommittee or to particular individuals, foul-ups can be traced and corrections instituted relatively quickly.

The most important "daily" routines—that is, tasks that on which a group must work consistently but are neither general meetings nor large-scale events—are (1) subcommittee and steering committee meetings, (2) phone calls and individual follow-up, (3) forum/general meeting preparation, (4) flyer preparation, (5) mailings, (6) leafletting, and (7) fund-raising work.

Subcommittees are almost always small groups of between three and ten people. They are usually highly task-oriented, with specific assignments for people to carry out. As the overall group has given the general direction for these subcommittees, the work can be much more directed without tremendous amounts of time being spent on membership orientation. (You would probably do this informally before the meeting with someone new.) Do not forget that people have joined the group to *do* things; they expect to see work here, not simply "communication." The way to socialize someone into the group is for everyone to be active, not just talkative.

Subcommittee meetings can be run formally if they are very large, but usually they don't have to be. While you need a chairperson to help direct the work and to keep to an agenda, be too rigorous in your formality here. If people are doing work, the work itself, by being concrete, puts limits on what is and isn't discussed. When wandering does occur, it is easy enough to get people back to business without a heavy procedural emphasis to the meeting.

Subcommittees need to show concret results. Objectives from previous meetings should therefore be the first items to be reviewed, with discussion on next stages of work occurring next. New objectives and tasks should be set as well, with subcommittee members taking specific responsibilities. If possible, join newer with more experienced members so that newcomers are not overwhelmed (and the group does not overestimate their commitment too quickly). Someone should be given formal responsibility for making a report or reports at the next general meeting or at the steering committee meeting.

A *steering committee* is the one ongoing committee that functions differently from other subcommittees (even though the manner of how it handles objectives and tasks is the same). It usually has the most committed activists on it; many of them will be "political" and may represent different political tendencies or distinct perspectives on issues within the group. The experienced and politicized nature of the steering committee's membership therefore necessitates a more formal agenda and consistently applied procedures.

Whether or not steering committees make "political" decisions for the group depends on what the group as a whole allows. It is my experience, however, that steering committees always have a large impact on the nature of every group, even when the overall group actively attempts to limit its responsibilities. The tremendous energy spent in grass-roots work makes this influence of a steering committee inevitable. However, influence can be checked by (1) formal group decisions to minimize policy discussions by any committee, (2) having clear guidelines for decision making on various issues, and (3) making certain that part of a steering committee membership is rotated every six months to a year, with no one serving more than two years in a row. This minimizes the power that accrues to certain long-term activists while guaranteeing widespread involvement by the membership. Of course, your group may live in a less ideal world than suggested by the above, and may want long-term experience in your formal leadership. Your group may also prefer to elect people on an openly political basis, regardless of longevity, believing that open political stances among the leadership are advantageous to the overall good of the group, minimizing potential manipulations that would otherwise occur. Either strategy has clear benefits and dangers that your group will have to assess—and thus represents a very important *political* decision.

These subcommittee (and steering committee) meetings should occur on the same weekday or night as the general meetings (say, Thursday). This way people learn to keep Thursdays open for your group function, be it a general, subcommittee, or steering committee meeting. You should never have more than two such *meetings* a week, preferably no more than one (except under intense periods of activism). People will otherwide become "meetinged-out," and the other work that needs to get done either will not be completed on time or will be too sloppily handled to be of much value.

One way around the problem of too many meetings while trying to complete other tasks is to "piggyback" a meeting on a work session concerned with mailing or flyer preparation (or the reverse). This way only one night is used for group activity, yet all the tasks are completed. This is especially applicable if the work described below is done in as social and pleasant an atmosphere as the activity allows.

PHONE CALLS AND INDIVIDUAL FOLLOW-UP

Do not assume that small things like phone calls can be put off until the last moment; in grass-roots organizations, that never works. Make your phone calls first: to see if the church is available: to three printers for comparative prices; to the two new members you want to make active and the one older one you want to keep that way. Phone calls can be short and quick, and putting them off makes grass-roots life more tension-provoking than it has to be. Even if you do not get through to your party, just knowing you made the effort and/or left a message that you called shifts the burden of responsibility slightly. Also, the phone calls often provide clarifying information (for instance, concerning the availability of a particular hall) that frees the group to move along.

Individual follow-up has been discussed earlier, but the need for it to be completed quickly needs to be underscored. People will be pleased and surprised if they hear you soon after a meeting. Your promptness also may activate them to scheduled subcommittee meetings, thus deepening their activism. If a phone call to a member is sufficient, do not request further follow-up, especially if you will see her or him at a subcommittee meeting. If a follow-up get-together does make sense, find out what is easiest for the person and try to accommodate. Such meetings, if held often, pack your schedule so tightly that you can never attend to other, nongroup issues that are part of weekly life, too.

FORUM/GENERAL MEETING PREPARATION

A forum of general meeting usually serves the two purposes of getting certain political business done while further involving and engaging members. Speakers and topics will be chosen with care, of course. However, do not assume a quick chat on the phone is sufficient when arranging for someone to speak will make her or his talk of clear benefit to your group. Remember to have a meeting or longer phone conversation with your speaker(s) beforehand to go over the topic and what is important for your group at the meeting. While the speaker can still say whatever he or she wants, the chances of it being unrelated to your needs should diminish.

Actually, the most important thing to take care of in planning a large meeting is finding a place in which to hold it. Once that is out of the way, a flyer can be completed even if you are not certain of a speaker. Without a place, no dates are definite, no flyers are possible—indeed, it is even difficult to engage a speaker. If you hold monthly meetings it is actually best to line up your meeting places two months in advance, so that the next meeting time and location can be announced at the end of each meeting—a quick and easy form of publicity.

If you are planning a forum or large event, it is best to have a specific subcommittee in charge of its details: sound system, chairs, tickets, literature sales, and so forth. Each item is small but often needs to be coordinated by someone who can keep on top of what can often snowball into an uncoordinated mess. So make certain the subcommittee is given full responsibility over such details, making everyone check with it before planning their own parts in the event. There are too many loose ends in grass-roots work without letting these get out of hand, too.

FLYER PREPARATION

Flyer preparation, as described in the previous chapter, is not as easy to do as it looks, especially if you want a good announcement or an attractive, eye-catching leaflet. Look over the specifics discussed in the last chapter. Always do this with someone else, especially someone you can train. Check out a number of printers before getting a flyer run off, making certain you get the best rates (which can vary tremendously). Do not be afraid to use different colors of paper if the price is not too high. All of these arrangements should be completed at least three weeks before the scheduled event.

MAILINGS

If your group decides to do a mailing, schedule the work session around three weeks before the event. (If you do it much earlier, people forget; much later, people are already booked up.) Make the mailing work session informal; accompany it with a pot luck dinner before or after, music, or the like. As for how to *do* the mailings, a few quick hints: fold flyers in bunches of fifteen to twenty, not one at a time; have a few sponges available to seal a group of five to seven envelopes at a time; use the sponges on stamps. If you want a bulk mailing permit to cut costs, do the mailing a month in advance of your meetings, since bulk mail moves *very* slowly. Above all, remember to enjoy yourself when doing these tasks by budgeting the time effectively and early enough to reduce time pressures and by making the work a semisocial event as well.

LEAFLETTING

Large institutions, when they need to publicize an event, do mass mailings, call press conferences[2] and are on the news the evenings preceding and following the event. They have a full-time public relations staff available to blanket an area as thoroughly as necessary with glossy posters, buttons, and programs. Grass-roots groups are not so fortunate. In place of highwired publicity, we use the leaflet— our own "two-page public relations department," as a friend once called it. Along with flyers and mailings, leaflets are our main publicity vehicle.

Do not distribute leaflets everywhere; rather, choose locations based on their importance to your group. Find out the hours when the number of people in the area will be greatest for (for example, at lunch, before or after work, or at the height of a rally). Work in teams so you cover people even if someone stops to talk (teaming also cuts down boredom in slack periods). Practice a convenient "handle" to attract people verbally. Do not take it as a personal affront when people express boredom or indifference. Leafletting is still pretty random; certainly the people are not expecting you. If they choose not to take a leaflet, it is their choice. If they should argue with you, do not get angry and argue vehemently back; state your position and then go back to your main task. Arguing while leafletting can only be counterproductive.

Finally, remember to have a pen and your organizer's notebook with you to sign up anyone who stops to chat and wants more information. After all, that's what leafletting is all about.

FUND RAISING

Grass-roots groups need money. All the time. Not only lots of it, but anything they can get. Ten dollars may pay for half the rent on a meeting hall; twenty dollars will buy a hundred stamps for a mailing. But a strange thing happens to many grass-roots organizers when they have to ask for money: they can't. Usually flowing out of things unrelated to the work itself (like guilt), this inability to ask confidently for funds leaves articulate men and women speechless before meetings or well-off potential contributors. This hang-up is a dead end and proves little. If you are proud of your group, you can confidently ask for money without shame—it is not going to be misused.

Therefore, every general or major event should have a request for "quiet donations" (the kind that don't rattle like coins, because they're paper). The requests are not to appeal to guilt but should be based on the responsibility to the group and the issues your group is involved in. By being proud of the work, you have no reason to be ashamed of the need for financial assistance. Indeed, to appear embarrassed is a tactical mistake that could create doubts where none existed.

Actual fund raisers for grass-roots groups are not that complicated. They need to be attractive enough so people will pay for what they have to offer. That means either really good entertainment (fine music, good food, and so on) or an important enough figure (or figures) to make the request for funds worth it. Consistent publicity in good locations and news spots well in advance of the event is important here. By being larger and more expansive than most meetings' publicity, the fund-raiser promotion creates an impression in people's minds of an event well worth the effort and expense, and this can nicely build momentum.

A *raffle*—either at the fund raiser or as a separate event—is also a good vehicle for raising funds. It can and does involve lots of members in an easy and satisfying manner that also publicizes the group. But make sure you have the people available to pound pavements and set up tables on street corners or at shopping centers before committing yourself to a raffle.[3] As the prizes need to be decent enough to entice people to enter, you need to know you can at least cover expenses before starting out. (Store owners can often be enticed to sell their products at cost for some free publicity on the raffle ticket.)

As with a forum subcommittee, the group needs a fund-raising committee to coordinate these tasks. You will want some people here who are efficient and who are good at record-keeping; others should be confident speakers who can ask for funds in a clear, comfortable manner. People from whom you request funds want to know how their money will be spent. They will ask questions, often hard ones. They will expect accountability and honesty. This committee will have to provide the answers and maintain the accountability if funding sources are to be maintained.

Of course, all of these problems diminish if you get a grant. *Everybody* wants a grant, so much so that I have come to believe that foundations and grant officers are the twentieth-century equivalents of "friendly visitors," only with more procedures. I cannot detail all that needs to be developed concerning grants; Armand Lauffer, among others, has developed an excellent guide for those interested.[4] Let me just say that (1) you need to be clear on what you want and how you plan to use the funds; (2) you need to show enough of your own resources where this addition of funds can be a catalyst for a significant increase in your group's effectiveness; (3) you need to document your request with evidence of good past activity (news articles, flyers, and so on); (4) you need a strategy to approach the correct foundation/funding source for your group (all funding sources are *not* alike); and (5) you need to write well. If you feel you can meet most of these requirements, get an appropriate fund-raisers' guide. Who knows? Perhaps your financial problems will decrease—until next year.[5]

All of this work—from setting up subcommittees to fund raising—is the essence of grass-roots activity. It will never be as efficient as that of large-scale organizations: Too many people forget something or have a personal problem that stops the work in its tracks, and there is never enough money or, seemingly, enough time. But the experience of working with like-minded people under these circumstances, as trying as those conditions can be, is rarely replicated in large-scale organizations. The chances that real bonds of friendship and comradely relations will be forged are quite high and can often last a lifetime. By approaching the work with foresight and realism and by engaging in the activity in as personable and sociable a manner as possible, you will find that the daily routines of grass-roots life end up being anything but routine—a delightful, ironic on what occurs in other organizations.

NOTES

1. Not that they are so terrific—it's just that their large resource base can allow numerous actions to go on at the same time, even when one or two members are not performing well. We have no such slack; when one person messes up, things stop.

2. Grass-roots organizations have press conferences, too. They will be discussed in Chapter 7, when we look at large demonstrations.

3. States vary on the regulations surrounding raffles, which you may want to check out before beginning.

4. Armand Lauffer, *Grantsmanship* (Beverly Hills, CA: Sage, 1978). For a review of other forms of fund raising, see Joan Flanagan, *The Grass Roots Fundraising Book: How to Raise Money in Your Community* (Washington, DC: The Youth Project, 1977).

5. To sharpen your skills in communications and publicity, see Marcia S. Joslyncherer, *Communication in the Human Services: A Guide to Therapeutic Journalism* (Beverly Hills, CA: Sage, 1979).

EXERCISES: DAILY ROUTINES

1. Subcommittee work for the coordinator or chairperson

   a. Do all subcommittee members have an assignment?

   b. Have you checked with each member a week before monthly meetings to see how the work is going? Does each subcommittee member have your phone number?

   c. Have new people been contacted and advised about the meeting, and has the potential assignment been explained to them clearly?

   d. Are materials ready?

   e. Have all written materials been given to members before the meeting, so time will not be wasted at the meeting itself?

2. Doing follow-up work

 a. Is there a list of people to call for this week? Do you have or does someone else have their numbers, and vice versa?
 b. Were follow-up calls needed with others? Did you or someone else contact them?
 c. What criteria did the group use for making follow-up assignments? Particular technical expertise, political sophistication, or personal factors? Or were no real criteria considered?

3. Checklist for special meetings and forums

 a. Has the meeting hall been seen for space, location, and so on?
 b. Are there enough chairs, tables, and electrical outlets?
 c. Is someone bringing refreshments?
 d. Is the agenda well prepared?
 e. Has someone reviewed speakers' responsibilities?
 f. Do the chairperson's skills match the needs of the audience?
 g. Are activists planning to be there one-half hour early for set-up and to help greet new people?
 h. Are sign-up lists prepared for attendance and for subcommittee assignments?
 i. Has part of the hall been set up adequately for child care?
 j. If donations are to be given, are cannisters clearly marked?

4. Flyer preparation checklist

 a. Remember—have the flyer and press releases ready one month in advance of your action or event!
 b. Has the time, place, and location been definitely secured?
 c. Do you have fresh, dark presstype and a dark typewriter ribbon on your typewriter?
 d. Will you use a graphic (like a cartoon)? Is it clear enough to show up once it has been run off?
 e. Did you call more than one printer on costs for running off the flyer?
 f. Is one side of the flyer as simple, graphic, and clear as possible? Is the motivation and justification for the event on both sides, or were you careful to limit one side's content to attract attention?

Chapter 6

MARCHES AND DEMONSTRATIONS

The most important contribution made by Harry Boyte's recent *The Backyard Revolution* was to dispel the illusion of a passive, indolent 1970s filled with disengaged, self-centered individuals.[1] The 1970s were hardly the 1960s in tempo, movement, or fun, but they did not lack for large numbers of committed people battling for progressive causes and issues they deeply believed in. Almost all of these grass roots groups, at one time or another, engaged in social-action events like demonstrations, rallies, and boycotts that had much of the fervor—if not the numbers—of the previous decade.

But why did such activity, if it had been fervent and important to so many people, receive so little publicity, be so little ingrained in the American consciousness? One could argue superficially that the media did not pay attention because the novelty had worn off, but that is ridiculous: They still cover the misery of Northern Ireland, the boredom of budget deliberations. Instead, growing attention has been paid to the Right—the conservative caucus, the Moral Majority, the Right-to-Lifers—because they now have more *power,* more influence over institutions in American life, and we don't. We may demonstrate and picket, but we now do so from a defensive and weakened position. Defensiveness, whether we like it or not, had better alter our *tactical considerations* (not our long-term objectives and goals) on how we plan social-action events, or we will continue to operate in today's weakened position.

This tactical consideration is not a call for an end to militancy, only for an effective use of militant tactics such as rallies and marches. Grass-roots groups need consistently (not constantly) to show their outrage and concern over existing conditions, and social-action events can be a timely, effective way to do so. Furthermore, it is impossible to predict when one social action event will spark a major upsurge capable of maintaining a mass movement. (For example, Poland's Solidarity activists spent years on small actions before a protest on meat escalated into a force capable of creating a social revolution). The consistent use of effective militant social actions, then, serves both the *immediately necessary purpose* of publicly speaking to issues that otherwise the larger public might never know about and the *longer-run, historical purpose* of maintaining a stance, however small, that contains within it the potential sparks needed for the larger social movements of the future.

That said, it is important not to confuse these two purposes. In the early 1980s it is necessary not to "make believe" you are part of some *mobilized* historical movement while forgetting the reality that your action will probably be small and little-noticed. If people are prepared for the likely (but not inevitable) minor outcome to their actions, they will not be demoralized when their event—whose energetic *form* is always suggesting so much more to every activist!—does not have the clout of the 1960s or 1930s.

One issue that must be faced is the problem of *too many demonstrations leading to activist burnout.* While the ideological and political reasons for this problem cannot be addressed here (although they will be touched on in the final chapter), your group will have to determine how to mesh its own needs with the increasing sense of urgency we all feel to go to *every* possible demonstration and rally. It does seem that a possible solution is developing, where broadly based, progressive groups focus on national days of action every six months (such as the September 19, 1981, AFL-CIO civil rights rally in Washington, D.C., called to protest the Reagan cuts) with more localized coalition actions that draw together people from a number of single-issue organizations. This two-tiered, less frantic approach seems more realistic, given our lessened resources, without sacrificing the dual purposes behind such actions that were mentioned above.

It is also possible for a scheduled social-action event to be more modest and yet more effective. First, a social action must be understood by the group as a tactic and not as an end in itself, a lesson poorly learned by many active in the 1960s. Today they are vehicles of publicity, morale-boosters, and an aid to sorting out groups with like interests and concerns. Alone they are not going to create victories unless they are part of a well-coordinated and planned strategy that contains many tactics of a collective and individual nature (such as political training, fact finding, and communication with other groups).

To succeed, a social-action event needs (1) a clear assessment of its real *and* potential resources, (2) a focused target, and (3) a program designed to attract as large a group as possible, given the particular commitments of the group.[1]

First, having a clear assessment of real and potential resources. As mentioned in an earlier chapter, an extremely well-publicized and institutionally based rally scheduled for May 1981 in New York called for a rally of 75,000 people to denounce the proposed federal budget cuts. Staff were given full time to mobilize the expected 75,-000, and expensive, attractive posters, leaflets, and mailings flooded every city social service agency and public sector trade union. Their reasoning for this huge turnout was deceptively simple: as these social welfare institutions and labor unions had a constituency of at least ten times that size, they expected to get 10 percent to the rally. But such a figure was based on one of two (or both) assumptions: (1) that an institution's catchment area or potential constituency perceives it with enough credibility to warrant a ready response, and (2) that there is enough agreement on the nature of the problem and how to fight it to warrant a *mobilized* response. For all our desire for such organizational legitimacy and political agreement, they do not yet exist, and our numbers will immediately reflect these twin realities. The 2,500 people that showed up for the May rally showed how disastrous it can be when one organizes on the basis of "hoped-for" rather than concrete numbers.

When grandiose expectations are dashed, inevitably a twofold process occurs: the rank and file are demoralized and increasingly cynical, lessening the likelihood of future involvement, and leaders too often become defensive and search for scapegoats (rarely themselves). Only if a thorough and honest scrutiny takes place where mistakes are admitted by the leadership and if the ranks are allowed greater involvement is it possible to come back quickly from this kind of defeat—a defeat that, since it does not have to occur, is all the more tragic. If you look at your actual, likely potential, and build publicity and momentum on that basis, the size of the turnout will less effectively be used against you by others and instead can be a boost for future work.

Second, focus on a concrete target. A major tactical error that has been made throughout the late 1970s and early 1980s has been the selection of overly broad and eventually hollow targets of attack. Fifty local rallies that attack the "Reagan administration" begin to lose their drawing power, especially as Reagan and Co., despite seemingly powerful rhetoric, are doing pretty much what they want. The large national demonstrations can provide this primary focus, but local actions, while not ignoring this larger reality, need to find targets that immediately and concretely affect people—and, by being smaller, have the potential to be affected in turn. For an example drawn from "the other side," anti-abortion activists at local levels often have gone after specific abortion clinics, specific legislators, local schools' educational programs, and so on. We need to target in a similar fashion: a hospital that stops abortion services, schools that may drop books from its curriculum, management's attempt to change work rules, and the like. These targets are small enough to change and yet embody the larger, systemic issues of the rightward advance that we all wish to reverse.

Third, a social-action event requires a clear political program. If a group is modest in assessing its resources and adroit in choosing its targets, it must also be *clear in what it is protesting in ways that attract people to the action and have the potential to engage them beyond it.* Do not shortchange yourself by being only localized or overburden yourself with large demands that cannot be met. A group (or groups) instead should range programmatic demands and concerns from the very local and concrete (some of which you may actually win) to larger, national, or systemwide concerns (which need to be addressed for long-term, political educational purposes).

Moreover, do not turn your social-action program and demands into a litany of the problems of the oppressed. (Again, this can be worked out at national demonstrations, where one has longer to deal with educational needs and where the overarching themes are, correctly, more all-embracing.) At a local level, only the most politically committed activists will see the tie-ins on, say, abortion rights, rent control, and foreign affairs in a way that they will be willing to turn out. Abortion rights, the ERA, opposition to violence, and protest against military expenditures have more meaning when several community and labor groups are working together. Each issue has a local and national focus (except the opposition to defense, which is a political statement) and can join large enough numbers of people around concrete, attainable objectives to make your action highly visible.

All of these issues are extremely important for human service workers, especially since more and more human service organizations are now entering the political arena in ways their official leadership once thought improper but now recognizes as necessary for organizational survivial. The attempt to "transform the social welfare state," as David Stockman recently put it candidly, has placed once well-off agencies in the kind of jeopardy that demands more activism.

Such action takes many forms—informal meetings with legislators and other officials, lobbying, and so on. Such techniques have been standard operations within social welfare for years. But the increased urgency now means that wider-scale, more militant activities like demonstrations and marches are acceptable tactics to human service leaders. At times this can create a quandary for activists who may be uncertain about their motives, but in fact such officially sanctioned activism can be a boon to wider-scale political activity if one approaches the work carefully.

First, it is likely that most agency-sponsored demonstrations will be moderately large, calling on broad participation of other official groups, unions, and mainstream civil rights organizations. The goals will be broadly etched in terms of attacking "the conservative tide" or "the Reagan administration." A demonstration's program will most likely contain a host of social welfare, union, and civil rights issues, carefully presented in ways that reinforce their own legitimacy and leadership. This breadth serves a purpose: It is general enough to attract larger numbers to promote their own strength, but not so targeted that it may antagonize local boards of directors, trustees, and the like.

These shifts in official activism tremendously increase a human service worker's potential for political effectiveness. As a human service worker, you may often have the right to participate in the planning of these rallies (suggesting better speakers, the type of march, and so on). You will have to assess your official leaders' openness to these suggestions, but my recent experience has found many more willing to experiment with ideas than would have been expected. This is especially true regarding speakers and endorsements, where someone you know from a progressive group may be able to make an excellent speech that presents your ideas to a broad audience.

If this planning avenue is closed to you, your grass-roots group or caucus should plan on having an attractive, clearly written leaflet for people to read and placards with solid slogans that are consistent with the march's principles but perhaps more sharply focused on issues you feel might otherwise be easily ignored. (This assumes you are not totally opposed to the march and how it is being handled; if you are, your placards may not be allowed by march officials. But constructive alternatives and ideas for action are usually acceptable.)

While agencies are much more open to political advice of all kinds today, highly specific, politically charged issues that have direct bearing on your agency's funding sources will most likely not be supported by the agency's leadership. (For example, antigentrification actions may affect a builder who sits on an agency's board of trustees.) This should not stop you from trying to involve others in your agency and the community in the action, but realistically the action will receive support from individuals at the workplace and not the workplace itself. However, just because the agency and its leadership do not become involved does not mean you cannot organize others to become engaged in the independent action sponsored by committed grass-roots groups. In doing so you may create broader community-*agency worker* coalitions that effectively push your own workplace into a more activist, progressive stance.

This background discussion of social-action events is necessary to clarify the distinctions between the changes wrought from the 1960s to today. The actual mechanics of social-action events are not that much different. Organizers often find them the most exciting and draining parts of their work. They are exciting because they encompass so many of the elements we know are part of large social movements: large numbers of people; genuine movement and concrete action; political demands coupled with the vision of a better world. These elements always touch the cadence, however slightly felt, of every march.

But marches can be so exhausting! We must plan what seems like a thousand details beforehand and then, once the march begins, we know that our actual control over what happens can be extremely limited. People come to marches and rallies for all sorts of reasons, and you cannot call a march to order as if it were a meeting. There may be some internal security, but crowd reaction to the march can only be

anticipated, not totally controlled. It can make people who pride themselves on thoroughness extremely anxious.

There is no answer to this problem, other than being thorough and
planning as well as possible by *involving as many people as possible
in the preparation.* This begins with collecting *endorsements* of the
action. A major error of the New York May rally organizers was that
endorsements were made by official leaders, not through any group
preparation. Once you have decided on an action, seek endorsements
at other group *membership* meetings: (1) where you work during
lunch or at group meetings, (2) trade union locals, (3) student govern-
ments; (4) community and neighborhood groups, and (5) religious
organizations. This means a lot of phone calling and footwork, but the
group discussions heighten the potential for group, not paper, support. After all, a 200-person rally that has been endorsed by forty
groups doesn't fool anyone, whereas 200 people from ten organizations means there are ten groups to be taken more seriously at the
local level.

Once endorsements have been made, the social-action committee
(probably made up of representatives from as many of these groups as
possible[2]) should choose an attractive time and route. The best times
for marches and rallies are either noon or around 5:00 p.m. during a
weekday (if you are trying to attract a workday crowd in a specific
area) or midday on the weekend (make certain it is not on or near a
holiday). The route will to a large extent be determined by your
chosen target, but if you are marching, do not make it longer than one
and a half miles (about thirty city blocks). It is important that the
route have good beginning and ending points. Marches rarely start on
time, so a symbolic, suggestive point of origin can be a helpful place to
begin building enthusiasm and start chanting.

You must also decide if your march route is designed for *symbolic
exposure* or *potential recruitment.* The former will emphasize places
and building sites that relate to the issue at hand; the latter is designed
to pick up people along the way. In either case, your group will have to
let the police know of your route well in advance; you must have a
parade permit and, at the rally point, a sound permit (one that allows
bullhorns or other sound equipment).[3]

Once your group has a decent number of endorsements, knows the
site and route of your social action, and has set a date, all the procedures spelled out in the previous chapter for leaflets apply. The
only thing that is different is that all publicity needs to begin around

two months before the scheduled action (unless it is based on an immediate crisis or there is a desire for minimal publicity). The bolder side of the leaflet should serve as your poster; this way people can recognize the event regardless of the publicity's form, thus increasing its visibility.

Postering is usually begun around one month before the date of the event. Naturally, you will work in teams—I suggest teams of eight working in pairs should blanket an entire targeted area at one time. If this ideal grouping is not possible, make certain you work in pairs; it's too sloppy to work alone. One person slops on the paste. (Evaporated milk squirted through a water "mister" is the best, followed by flour and water, with wallpaper paste a sticky third.) The other puts on the poster. (If you have to do this alone on a windy day, it is a mess!) Do not use staples—they make it too easy for your poster to be ripped down. Ask neighborhood businesses to post signs in their windows, too.

Leafletting should begin about the same time, but the main "leaflet blitz" takes place in the last two weeks, after the posters have been in place and the mailing to organizations has been completed. (You may want to poster again, if you have the resources.) This leafletting can also be used to see how well known the event is, how interested in the issue people are, and so on. Furthermore, all of this work itself is an excellent test to see which of the endorsing groups have been serious about their support and which have not. The selection of speakers would reflect the difference.

Press releases are usually sent out ten days to a week before the actual event. (That means the press release must be ready to mail *before* the previous week). Plan a follow-up phone call the *morning* of the event. The first of these calls should be to the Associated Press and United Press International wire services, because their teletypes serve as major information sources for all other media. If specific reporters or correspondents are known to individuals, they should be contacted after the press release has been sent (send them one, too).

The press release should be short, dramatic, and informative. The first paragraph, worded for punch, should list the action, time, and place. The second paragraph should briefly describe why the action is being called and who is expected to attend; name important figures and endorsing groups to heighten media interest. The third paragraph should state what you expect to happen (be dramatic but not grandiose), briefly placing the event in strategic context. A final, two-line paragraph, giving the name and phone number of a contact person, completes the press release. Its entire length should never be longer than one page of typed, double-spaced copy—it is not by accident that media people call press releases "throw aways." By suggesting urgency and real activity in a concise form, the press release increases the likelihood of the event not being "thrown away". So don't bore the reader. If you want, enclose flyers that will explain more once he or she is interested.

You may want the press release to announce not only a social-action event but also a press conference. If this is so, hold the press conference as close to the event as logistically possible, either the morning before or the morning of the event. A good hour is 11:00 a.m., because it is early enough to make all afternoon paper, rush-hour radio, and the evening news. The press conference must emphasize the most dramatic or interesting parts of the event: newsworthy speakers, genuinely *new* information, or something exciting about the event that will increase its public interest (street actions, civil disobedience, and the like).

Hold the press conference in a place that is convenient for the press to reach (assignments, especially on the weekend, are often based in part on their accessibility), yet financially feasible for the sponsoring group. Have a microphone and your own tape recorder available at a front podium that faces toward the reporters. If possible provide coffee and donuts; developing good relations with particular reporters never hurts. However, *do not* call a press conference separate from the rally unless it serves some purpose organic to the group; it is a publicity vehicle that can work only if there is a reason to give the *conference* visibility beyond the rally itself. That tactical decision is one each social-action event steering committee will have to make for itself.

All of this work is preparation for the event itself. One of the most important work groups involved in the event is security. "Security" is a harsh-sounding word for what today is usually the group of parade marshals needed to keep people moving, lead the chants, and, if necessary, keep people in line in ways the group has previously decided are acceptable. These marshals should be drawn from the groups that have been *actively* involved in the planning of the event. Rules should be gone over, distinctive, single-colored armbands distributed, and procedures of accountability and communication set up (concerning who the press should see for official comments, who has the medical equipment and so on).

The march itself will begin thirty to forty-five minutes later than its announced time, so plan your schedule accordingly. Marshals and others involved in logistics should be there an hour early. They need a final run-through on the route, should be given a firm commitment as to the actual starting time, and can serve as an attraction for people arriving. They, in turn, can expect to answer people's questions about departure time, who will be at the rally, and so forth. This is why their information needs to be clear and correct; otherwise, their future authority is undermined.

Those in charge of chants and slogans (often a good part of the security staff) should have a 5½ x 8½-inch leaflet to distribute to marchers to help with the chants. The leaflet's size will distinguish it from all other leaflets and can be held easily in one hand while marching under any weather conditions. The chanters will undoubtedly be volunteers, but make certain they are not hesitant, retiring types. There is nothing worse to the ear than a militantly phrased chant being tepidly led, so make certain your chant leaders are verbally expressive. (Here is an excellent opportunity for young and enthusiastic members to perform a valuable task.)

If the march or demonstration is to conclude with a rally, those who will be speaking at the rally should march as well. There is no reason one group should "lead" by rhetoric while the others "follow" through the hard work of a long march. Seeing leaders march like everyone else, as Malcolm X and Martin Luther King knew well, helps build an important bond among all members of a movement. Those in charge of the rally coordination should stay at the rally site, of course. But that is because of their tasks, not their titles.

While others are planning to march, the rally subcommittee should above all else make certain that the sound system is in working order. Too many only work halfway through a program. Have tested personnel involved here; the work is technically difficult and can only be dealt with well by people who are mechanically competent. They should have a car and a little cash readily available for the missing wiring, fuses, or batteries that seem always to be needed at the last minute.

Ideally, I believe, a rally should mix music and/or theater (short, comedic skits, pantomime, and the like) with a few speakers chosen by the groups involved. Speakers will undoubtedly represent the political composition of the group, but each should be asked to address certain themes that complement rather than parallel each other. There is nothing worse (or, unfortunately, more common today) than hearing six speakers all address the same topic in the same way, attacking the same enemies, making the same demands, proposing the same solutions. Some speaker(s) should emphasize the context of the rally, others should describe the current problems and needs, and still others should propose potential solutions. While there is always overlap, the particular emphasis lends a thematic coherency to the rally without turning it into a drone-in. Each speaker should be asked to speak for a certain number of minutes, with the main speaker(s) getting more time. Try to get the speakers to understand and agree to the time limits well beforehand. The sight of a large crowd in a public place seems either to unnerve some people, reducing them to monosyllabic brevity, or to inspire others to talk longer than ever imagined. Be prepared!

The rally coordinator should introduce speakers and serve as a conduit for information, giving pertinent announcements along the way on an as-needed basis (mentioning where literature tables are or reading telegrams of support). He or she should make certain that the last few speakers (as well as the main speaker) mention the ongoing work beyond the rally and make requests for donations and new recruits. These latter functions, which relate to the long-term effectiveness of the groups larger strategy, need to be well coordinated. Place information tables in prominent spots, and give specially marked marshals the responsibility to circulate with rally canisters for donations.

The rally should be the culmination of the social action's objectives. It is important that the groups spell out their larger strategic expectations, letting people know of the other actions and concerns of the event's sponsors. This way newcomers can consider getting involved in what appears to be an ongoing and dynamic group, albeit necessarily modest, that is fighting to stop the rightward advance. If these social actions are carried out well, modest resources and objective defensiveness need not greatly hinder the progress of your group. People understand these realities; what they need to see are effective mechanisms that are fighting to reverse present trends in ways that make sense to them. Over time, the successful growth of your organization through the momentum-building nature of all your tactics will instill enough confidence in people to stay active and committed to the work that lies ahead. And as that happens, the even wider-scale changes becomes more and more possible.

NOTES

1. Thus, a single-issue group with a pluralist political perspective would try to build the event as large as possible, regardless of other group differences. Another group with a more leftist or nationalist perspective would be more limited in size, due to its more sharply etched program, but clearer in its political and programmatic direction.

2. Do not select all your speakers until the steering committee has been seen in action—it's the place to see who is truly committed and who is not.

3. Unless your group has decided it wishes to confront this police authority, which makes the issue of permits superfluous.

DEMONSTRATION PLANNING GUIDE

Agency-sponsored demonstrations: Broadly based, institutionally focused in outreach; more general goals and targets.

Grass-roots-organization—sponsored demonstrations: Either issue-specific or broadly based, but focused on individual and group outreach with more specific targets and goals.

Planning:

1. Choice of issues and slogans around which to call the demonstration.

2. Sponsorship.

3. Outreach: what groups will receive mailings, posters, speakers; who will be called individually?

4. What is the line of march or place of rally? What is the most advantageous route? Does the rally spot have any political significance? Do you have permits?

Publicity:

1. Leafletting: Plan and coordinate most opportune locations for leafletting two weeks in advance; leaflet over that time period.

2. Posters: They should be distributed and placed over the three-week period preceding rally.

3. Press release: Send a press release ten days in advnce and follow up with phone calls the day of the action.

March Activity:

1. Prepare placards, costumes, music, and other march paraphernalia.

2. Chants should be mimeoed on small pieces of paper for marshals to distribute.

3. Marshalls need to be trained the night before (at least) on the route, legal requirements, and, for some, how to chant.

Rally Preparation:

1. Rally coordinator should have legal permits in hand at all times.

2. Speakers should be consulted on their talks a week in advance.

3. Have literature tables up before marchers arrive.

4. All rally marshals should have sign-up sheets in abundance.

5. Fund-raising cannisters should be distributed and clearly identified.

6. The clean-up crew should be in action as soon as the march and rally are over.

Chapter 7

COALITION WORK

As was suggested in the previous chapter, many agencies are willing to sponsor, or at least see the need for, social-action events. The committees that plan these events are often viewed as "coalitions" or multiorganizational groups. As long as the coalition focuses on one *short-term* event and that event alone, such groupings usually work relatively well, for there are fewer "hidden agendas" of a political or organizational kind for one to worry about. In general, few human service agencies will be found officially in other coalitions (except the ongoing legislative coalitions that have existed for years). Such a move on their part would suggest a shift in overall strategic direction.

But for many human service workers who see the long-term direction of events in our society as needing some consistent response, these strategic, multiorganizational considerations can take on much more importance. The groups with which one works in such coalitions tend to be more grass-roots based, ranging from union caucuses, women's groups, single-issue formations such as pro-ERA or anti-nuclear groups, to community neighborhood organizations. These formations demand that activists be savvy as to how coalitions can be run successfully, for political strategy—with all its nuances—is the essence of such groups.

That said, there's no getting around it: Coalitions are almost always a painful experience for grass roots organizers.[1] Whether they should be is another matter, but coalition work is "permanent pain," as a well-seasoned veteran of the New York movement experience put it.

Coalitions exist in part because every group is too weak to function alone, at least on certain issues. Their existence, while drawing together a wide range of activists, is often a constant, slightly irritating reminder of how much we have to build.

Likewise, at least one-half of coalition life is formed by the "hidden agendas" of the various groups participating in them. Beneath the surface calm of some relatively straightforward meetings lurk many organizational pushes and pulls to assert influence or increase power. For the inexperienced organizer, coalition life is too often a pummeling lesson in organizational politics; for the more experienced, it is simply long, hard work.

The divisions will manifest themselves in different forms, regardless of the political stance of the overall coalition itself. More traditional agencies and grass-roots organizations develop hidden agendas because too many of them have operated too competitively with each other in the past. They have too often attempted to enlarge their own organizational turf or further the careers of their leaders, regardless of other organizations' potential involvement or legitimate claims. On the other hand, more progressive organizations' hidden agendas flow out of their constant attempts to dominate a coalition *politically,* thus proving the "correctness" of their "political lines" (on how to wage the struggle) and enhancing their reputations among new and potential recruits to the group.

I am not suggesting that *all* groups function in these two ways. Most do not. But it takes only one or two such organizations in any coalition to subvert its potential and misdirect its external course of action. The 1970s and early 1980s are strewn with the wreckage of many fine community and labor coalitions that were destroyed by such divisiveness. Few have lasted a year; many that have are coalitions in name only, dominated by one group or another. Such wreckage is a reflection of the disarray and weakness in which we now find ourselves. We therefore must admit to such division if we ever are to heal quickly enough for the fight that lies ahead.

Given this painful reality, people who enter coalitions should work to minimize the dominance of any one group while pushing the coalition itself to confront actively the tasks it has set for itself. This twofold task of *organizationally limiting any individual dominance while seeking to expand collective action* means that at least some of your group's representatives must be very experienced if you are to be truly effective. How to tell when someone is pushing for her or his group's "line dominance" or "organizational control" will not be learned overnight.

It can all be very complicated. For example, back in 1978 some very involved, motivated people in New York set up a support coalition for the miner's strike. Some of the most active people began suggesting that the New York support caravan, which was part of the national network established by the miners, should make an extra stop in Pennsylvania. The caravan members would need a rest, with some publicity it would help the cause, and there were a number of miners there who would appreciate the support. The plan seemed excellent to almost everyone, until they learned from a few experienced organizers that the stop was in the one town where the above individuals' political group had real dominance. To have stopped there would have signaled to the West Virginia miners, already burned by the organization in 1976, that the New York coalition was controlled by that same political group—an incorrect perception that would nevertheless have been damaging to the coalition's reputation. It all seemed so minor, but if some organizers had not been politically familiar with the group's political history, the motion would easily have passed and destroyed the coalition.

Coalition life needn't be fraught with such subtle sabotage, especially when there is original widespread agreement on both the problem or issue confronting the coalition and how best to attack it. Achieving such unanimity necessitates two very solid principles to guide any coalitional effort: (1) agreement that the coalition use political discussion, especially at the initial (two or three) meetings to thrash out the definition and limits to the coalition's "politics"; and (2) a norm of activity that necessitates ongoing, *active* commitment to the coalition as the basis of a group's or individual's credibility as a coalition member.

Political discussion needs to go on at every coalition meeting, but it is perhaps most important in early meetings, where the groundwork is set for what the coalition is about, how it makes decisions, and what its choice of tactics will be. For if you are successful, the coalition will grow, and new participants (of every political stripe, from willing and naive to closed and sectarian) will want to know the norms of behavior, basis for joining, and types of tactical options. If there are clear and well-established guidelines that have been democratically decided early on, future sabotage will not get far, while others will learn the nature of broad-based decision making.

The most important part of the political discussion will be on the "statement of purpose" or "program in brief." Its four parts include (1) definition of the problem and its causes; (2) definition of the group and its general character, in terms of potential membership, class, and sexual and racial makeup; (3) strategic direction for coalition actions; and (4) the basis of specific membership in the coalition.

None of these issues can be thrashed out easily. As Jack Rothman pointed out in "Three Models of Community Organization Practice,"[2] each of these topics can be categorized into very different types of outcomes, depending on a membership's political inclinations. A citywide coalition that purposely decries, say, only the problem of recent layoffs in the auto industry might sight the Reagan administration's policies and foreign imports as the problem. The coalition's general character would be open to everyone who wished to fight imports and the Reagan administration, while the strategic direction would emphasize traditional forms of legislative reform. Specific membership would be determined on a voluntary basis.

However, the above formation would be sharply different if you added the simple political statement that the layoff problem is endemic not only to the Reagan administration but to the way all our economic and political leaders have handled auto worker problems. Suddenly, the issue of class enters the nature of the problem. Furthermore, the role (or lack of one) by the trade union leadership in fighting the layoffs may begin to enter into the debate. This could then mean a move away from a reliance on traditional legislative reform activity to "bottom-up" rank-and-file activity at the workplace or in the community, with correspondingly tighter demands on the coalition membership.

These examples may sound like a potential quagmire, and there is no denying they can be. But these are the kind of tricky issues involved in coalition life that we need to face. Beneath these debates there is also a sifting process going on, a process whereby political ideas are explored and tested in ways that will allow for greater cohesion among today's divided progressive grass-roots organization in the future. So do not avoid the debates if you decide that these formations are needed. The problems certainly will not go away!

So the arduous political process of answering these hard questions must be gone through early on in the coalition's existence (indeed, there will be need for consistent political discussion). But equal in importance to political discussion is the testing of individual and group commitment to the coalition through people's ongoing activity. Every coalition has its political entrepreneurs and facile political analysts, *but do they produce?* Do they perform the functions the coalition has set out, or do they march to their own sectarian or individualistic drummer? My personal experience is that I would prefer to work with someone with whom I have honest political disagreements who nevertheless puts the coalition's policies in action (once debate is finished) than with some summer soldier who rhetorically supports all the "correct actions" but hasn't the energy to work. Go through political debate, but suspend some of your judgments until you see everyone in action. Likewise, the coalition itself, if it is to limit the cyclical trek of rhetorical leaders and sectarians to a "one-shot" visit, must have a part of its statement of purpose that members must "actively participate in some supportive way" in the actions of the coalition and/or its subcommittees.[3]

You can never know or have answers to these issues until the coalition has been in operation for a number of months. It could fall apart, or jell nicely into a well-coordinated body. But you cannot know until ideas and the people behind them have proved their worth in activity.

STRUCTURAL ISSUES

The initial steering committee will probably be voluntary and therefore should function for a limited time period before actual elections are held. Its voluntary nature is inevitable, since people will have little immediate basis for serving on it, unless there is a sponsoring group or groups involved from the inception. (Even then you will wish to cast your net widely to ensure broad participation.) The basis for initial service should be (1) agreemnt with the statement of purpose, (2) a willingness to take at least partial responsibility for an area of coalition work, and (3) a defined constituency or group that is part of the coalition's overall constituency.

This steering committee should be in place for about three months. That is a long enough time to sift through who is sincerely working for the good of the group, who politically supports the coalition, what skills and resources people have, and so on. The entire coalition membership can then elect a steering committee to serve for a longer period, usually about a year (or until the coalition's task is done, if it is less than a year).[4]

Of course, in discussing elections we get to the issue of who is a member of your coalition. Regardless of what your political perspective is, I believe that once a coalition has been established, *voting* members must have attended at least two previous meetings in some predetermined time period (three to four months) and in some way have *actively* supported the work of the group. These requirements cannot apply in the formation of the coalition itself, obviously, but need to be developed around the time of the steering committee election. These requirements weed out both the sectarians, who are there only to criticize, and the opportunists, who are there only to use the coalition's name.

While it is important not to be dogmatic in your approach to such requirements (active "support" may be distributing the newsletter where someone works), the necessity of some test through *activity and general political agreement and understanding* has been shown to be a sine qua non for healthy coalition life. As said before, it serves as a sifting process. Furthermore, it is a form of protection for those with minority political positions on different strategic issues who nevertheless function in a principled and honest way. If active and generally supportive of the "statement of purpose," such people cannot be railroaded out by others seeking to "cleanse" a coalition of internal difference. Internal differences are a reality of grass-roots life today, for no one is certain of our entire future course of action. We therefore need to accept them without sacrificing our commitments to overall, unified political action and momentum within the coalition.

As difficult as the above discussion suggests this work can be, it is important here to reiterate why this must be so. Coalitional activity serves many purposes. On one level, it attempts to get certain concrete political tasks accomplished (those related directly to the issues themselves). On another level, it serves as a testing ground for various proposed strategies that coalition members thrash out together before setting a course of action. Finally, the work sifts out those who are genuinely committed from those good at lip service, preparing and legitimating the reputation of individuals and groups for future leadership roles.

These three functions increase the importance of an honest and thorough scrutiny of strategies and objectives once an action has been completed. I am *not* talking here about an endless routine of criticism/self-criticism at every meeting, but of a healthy assessment at periodic intervals where shortcomings are discussed and successes supported in ways that constructively move the coalition ahead. This is part of the way we learn to overcome the larger social divisions that confront us in grass-roots work, so do not hurry through this in order to move on to some other action.

This is why coalition life needs its democratic structure, its testing through activity, and its limited but real internal membership criteria that protect the entire coalition while guarding political minorities' rights. When it works well, as ACORN demonstrated in Arkansas in the late 1970s, the limited resources of grass-roots organizations are expanded and political clarity is increased, cementing deeper alliances for the future.[5]

We need to look on all such coalitions as still fragile but valuable arenas where we see the state of social movements today, *not as we need them but as they are.* We cannot expect these coalitions to substitute for that larger movement we want—which would lead to vanguard posturing of the worst sort—but we can respect them (and their members) for the work actually going on. With more modest aims reflective of our presently weakened position, the three purposes mentioned above can be accomplished.

NOTES

1. The only written example of coalition development I have seen is the already out-of-date "Coalition Formation and Development," by Joyce C. Welsh, in *A Guidebook for Local Communities Participating in Operation Independence* (Washington, DC: National Council on the Aging, 1975).

2. Jack Rothman, "Three Models of Community Organization Practice," in Cox et al., *Strategies of Community Organization* (Itasca, IL: Peacock, 1978).

3. "Supportive action" cannot be overdone, either, where people must put aside all work in their own groups for the coalition. "Support" must range from wide-scale activity to the distribution of the newsletter or attending a rally. To do otherwise is to substitute politics for action alone, a blind form of organizing that helped destroy parts of the student New Left in the late 1960s.

4. If the time limits are shorter, the earlier voluntary period should reflect that difference.

5. Andrew Kopkin, "ACORN Calling: Door-to-Door Organizing in Arkansas," *Working Papers,* 1975, Vol. III, No. 2.

EXERCISES: COALITION ACTIVITY

1. Is this a long-term or a short-term coalition? If it is long-term, assume that the demand for political strategy skills are greater.

2. Does the coalition steering committee provide work for interested members right away? Who actually does the work, as opposed to only talking? Does your coalition need a work requirement for membership?

3. Are there people who only bring their own group's literature to the meeting? If they do, why? Do they also carry out the tasks of the coalition?

4. Do those with minority opinions who work hard for the coalition receive the same rights as those who hold dominant positions?

5. Does the coalition have membership requirements to avoid the "packing" of meetings, or is such a tactic unnecessary?

6. Are people elected to the steering committee? How long are their terms? Or does the group emphasize volunteers and open-ended terms?

The more easily and clearly you can answer these questions for long-term coalitions, the less likely that your group is unprepared for potential political discord. However, if this a short-term coalition, the more emphasis on these issues, the less focused the coalition probably is on outside work. Finally, if such matters drag on in a coalition for over six months, the less likely the coalition will survive.

Chapter 8

DEMOCRACY AND EQUALITY
Fighting Bias Inside the Organization

As I have learned recently, grass-roots organizing is a lot like parenting: It is a lot easier to discuss and analyze the concrete difficulties than it is to share the joys with those who have not experienced them. Lack of sleep, the never-ending clean-up, and the quick adjustments to unforeseen accidents are common to both experiences and easily understood by anyone. But the joy, because it is often so quiet and intuitive, does not lend itself as easily to the printed or spoken word.

Still, joy there is, sometimes in the magnificence of major strategic victories, other times in the simple, comradely way in which a few people, having banned together, come to respect and trust each other in work well done. For "good work," as anyone who has gone through organizing knows, need not translate into major strategic victories to have been a real success.

What makes this irony about success so real will be found in the nature of organizing itself. It is one of the few arenas in American life where there is genuine potential to share a real egalitarian and democratic experience. Workplaces are structured to limit this experience and seek new ways to continue the trivialization of worklife.[1] Other institutions, from schools, families, and trade unions to religious organizations, give better lip service but little real support to an egalitarian method of working and sharing. Such problems are even worse if you are a women or a member of a racial minority.

Grass-roots organizations, for all their creaky structures, intense meetings, and overstretched resources, can be quite different. Regardless of the conservatism of the larger society, many such organizations serve to train people in that increasingly rare experience of self-determination: people learning they have a right to "make history,"[2] to choose how they will act, given the particular context in which they live. Such training is vital today, for it creates people skilled and confident enough to help lead the needed wide-scale social movements of tomorrow.

I relearned how important this training has been as I worked on this book. As I reviewed my own organizing experiences, sorting out errors and advances, checking on others' work and rereading much of the organizing literature, I saw how important genuine democratic, egalitarian functioning was in determining the success of so many strategies and plans. The successes were not only those where groups gained materially, but also those where objective gains were blocked but people decided to carry on anyway.

Again and again, rank-and-file democracy seemed essential. But "democracy" does not mean simply voting. That lesson on "participatory democracy" that many of us practiced in the 1960s— having "all-night meetings so *all* participated on *every* decision"—turned into a form of elitism, since only the most committed (usually those without jobs or family responsibilities) could "participate." As the previous seven chapters have suggested, the forms of democracy that lead to self-determination for group members involve not only voting but at least the following *three* issues:

(1) *The breaking down of artificial status and/or heightened divisions between leaders and members through a sharing of all grassroots organizational maintenance responsibilities.* Most institutions use the advancement to leadership as a move away from involvement in daily routines concerned with organizational maintenance. The assumption here is that leaders need only "think" and plan larger, more important decisions, while followers execute, usually without thought and rarely with adequate feedback to the top. Grass-roots organizations can and often do break the subtle but quite powerful socialization message of elitism by having everyone in some way involved in mailings, clean up, postering, and so on. In this way the ranks see the human side of the leaders and the leadership never loses sight of the ranks' value to the organization. Here the socialization message is quite different: While differences in function, knowledge,

and responsibility exist, all functions, knowledge, and responsibilities—and the people associated with them—are important to the organization. Rather than feeling less valued over time, people come to feel the reverse.

Second, "expertise" is not simply the formal kind that involves regulated training (with all the class, racial, and sexual bias that often accompanies it), but both informal and formal. *Furthermore, it is the ongoing practice of that expertise, not simply the expertise alone, that legitimizes one's authority in the group.* Being a lawyer will matter if you have been a lawyer whose services have been consistently available to the group. Likewise, the woman without a high school diploma who has become a housing expert will have far more authority than other lawyers because she has learned and developed her skills for the group's overall good. These grass-roots norms that place high value on informal, experiential skills and that grant trust only on the basis of *consistent* practice are of tremendous benefit in both the breaking down of old, elitist myths and the creation of new, egalitarian ones.[3] It is part and parcel of the demystifying of what is and is not skill, of what is democratic leadership versus hierarchical authority, what warrants respect rather than awe. Such values and the attitudes and behaviors they engender in people are the bedrock of the grass-roots tradition, which we need to refine even more throughout the 1980s.

Third, if it is possible, we must structure grass-roots organizations in ways that develop an understanding of "bottom-up" accountability and decision making without necessitating a loss in organizational effectiveness. The importance of a steering committee bringing policy decisions to membership meetings lies in the creation of self-respect in the membership itself. That these people have an organization in which they have the *right* to set the basic strategies of what and how things get done is a powerful antidote to the way other institutions function. Likewise, the subcommittee structure of grass-roots groups goes beyond creating a division of labor. Subcommittees are a training ground for new skills. The mixing of new and more experienced members on such committees makes possible the creation of new talent and the refining of old. As leaders are held in less sanctified positions of authority and status exists less by rank than through concrete activity, these structural arrangements increase the mixing of ideas and skills in ways that most other organizations actively disallow. "Democracy," instead of meaning little more than the solitary act of voting, comes to mean within grass-roots groups the essence of purposeful self-determination: *People actively believe* they have the right to make and take responsibility for decisions that affect their lives. In the 1980s, such beliefs are not simply political but serve as the basis for a genuine alternative to the conservative status quo. But the preceding discussion speaks to the genuine structural and procedural *potential* within groups. There is another reality to grass-roots life that must be addressed if "potential" is to translate into the concrete reality of everyday grass-roots functioning: the continuation, often unconscious, of racism, sexism, and class bias within many grass-roots groups.

Let me say immediately that many of these biases are not intentional; indeed, they often occur inside groups genuinely devoted to fighting such problems. But just as we *all* have been socialized not to expect or, at times, even want genuine democracy,[4] we all have been socialized within a society where racism, sexism, and class bias are prevalent. We cannot get rid of such biases simply because we wish to or because we do not like them. It takes almost as much effort to overcome them within our groups as it does to banish them from society as a whole. We will have to continue struggling with these issues for a long time to come.

One part of our "internal" battle can be effectively waged by learning about and coming to respect fully different cultural traditions. Understanding the undermining effects of racism and sexism through a systematic study of history must be undertaken by anyone personally concerned with these issues. Organizations can set up classes and study groups. The best results usually occur under the direction of individuals directly affected by bias and prejudice—say, women or Blacks. These people will, understandably, lead the way as teachers, but we must recognize that responsibility must lie with all of us. This is because the eradication of racism, sexism, and class bias is in everyone's self-interest. If those of us who are fighting our biases fail to perceive this fact, our intentions as "students" will not be trusted, and the social leaders in this area are more likely to be relegated to token positions within the organization. Therefore, while your study group's reading lists and themes of inquiry may be based on suggestions from women or Blacks, the responsibility of carrying out the work, completing the readings, and wrestling with the issues must be with those in the study group itself.

But this is just one relatively simple structural addition a group can make. If you are wondering how effective you and your organization are in resolving some of the underlying social tensions within your group, try to answer the following questions. Use your "gut" and not your head here, for it is always possible to rationalize away problems with the "press of circumstances" excuse: There wasn't enough time for that extra training; distance isn't for social but geographic reasons; and so on. Each excuse may be understandable; what you have to decide is whether these singular instances add up to a subtle but nevertheless present form of bias.

Are you and/or others at times surprised by "color-blind" or "sex-blind" skills exhibited by certain members? When a Black person speaks knowingly of housing law and not just slumlords, how do you react? Are you "pleasantly surprised"? Do you find you check out their assertions more often than those of white counterparts? Likewise, if a woman is assertive and forceful in successfully engineering a complex campaign, do you feel she is just a bit too aggressive, that she is doing this work to make up for "lost" personal needs?

Are people of different social characteristics allowed to make errors or achieve successes in the same terms as middle-class white males? When mistakes are made—and remember, they are being made by us all, often—do they register in a collective way ("See, women just are not ready for that kind of responsibility") or in individual terms ("Susan did well in the overall planning of the strategy, but needs to work on some parts of executing it, especially publicity and media work"). The latter, individualized critique allows a *person* to grow; the former, unconsciously collective condemnation leaves little room except for others' self-fulfilling prophecies of eventual failure. Likewise, if the leadership of such people is treated as more "special" than it really is, its burden of "greatness" can only create a combination of social distance from others and a gnawing sense of being seen as more perfect than they inwardly know they are. Such tensions, while cloaked in the guise of perceived brilliance and achievement, in fact form a blueprint for eventual discord, animosity, and failure.

Do you and other group members have a mix of friends among the group's co-workers, or do they tilt in one social direction? I am not talking about loving everyone you work with; that notion died or some commune in either Colorado or Vermont around 1971. And one isn't expected to deny one's social characteristics or live the incorrect fantasy that "we're all alike," either. But are you and other group members comfortable with others where a social mingling can and does take place over time? If so, this suggests a comfort with and respect for *difference* that allows you to relax and enjoy people as people—with differences and similiarities—and not just as social categories that fulfill certain functions and perform certain token tasks for the group as a whole.

Finally (and perhaps most tellingly), is it possible to have a serious disagreement with someone else and not have it perceived as a racial/sexual division? Do you hedge a disagreement too much to smooth things over, even though you then stew about it for weeks after (all the while getting angrier, knowing that your initial reticence was because of *social difference,* not because you *felt* less argumentative). This is one of the hardest problems to overcome, for a respect for difference also carries with it the necessity of initial temperance on arguments and ideas as people work together to locate and develop a common point of reference. That working and testing process necessarily goes on in any group. But at some point after working together there must be a shift toward not only common understanding but everyday discourse that values and displays enjoyment of disagreement as a necessary ingredient in grass-roots democratic life. Without that, a lot of benign posturing is simply an easily crumpled masquerade.

You can create at least three structural elements and two personal ones to help overcome some of these problems. First is the group's genuine commitment to ongoing work on these problems. Women, Blacks, Latins, gays, and others will have a lot more tolerance for a group and its members if they actively and genuinely try to overcome social injustice than they will for those who give little more than lip service. Second, the classes and study groups must be developed and integrated as a serious part of the organization's life. They may not come to dominate, but this concrete show of a desire to *learn* (which is a lot more than "showing" concern) is a measure certain to enhance a group's reputation.

Finally, there must be a mechanism of group scrutiny that fairly analyzes progress on these issues as much as they do on other parts of a group's functioning. Criticism/self-criticism may work, but it often has been used as either a soapbox or a punching bag. If the evaluation is not elevated to a separate (and overly intense) status beyond other

points of examination (such as leadership accountability, staff functioning, and campaign effectiveness) *from the beginning,* then there
can be a decent chance for group success. But if a group waits until
problems occur before instituting such procedures, there is little
likelihood that it will ever achieve its objectives of better social
integration and respect throughout its diverse membership.

There are also two personal points to follow. *First, do not hide who
and what you are; be yourself.* This may sound simplistic, but it isn't.
This kind of tactical self-awareness (see Chapter 2) necessitates an
internal knowledge and comfort with whatever your class, racial, and
sexual origins are. Talk in a style that is *you,* not what you think you
ought to be. Dress in your style, recognizing and respecting cultural
differences when you travel to other groups' meetings or enter others'
homes. Do not be embarrassed if you went to college or beyond; *do* be
embarrassed if you think advanced degrees are a measure of natural
intelligence. Do not hide skills; rather, make them available for the
use of the group. The last thing a grass-roots group needs today are a
lot of like-minded, "aw shucks, we're all alike and you know more
than me anyway" simpletons. Poor and working-class people certainly know this. So practice your *skills,* rather than developing a
politically correct persona for some imaginary organizer that you will
never be. Developed naturally, your style will help you find that you
are a better and more respected organizer than you might have
thought possible.

Second, do not simply identify with oppressed people, but identify
similiar circumstances in your own life and the behaviors and feelings
they breed in you. Trace those circumstances in your life that made
you feel different, outside, an object, and remember what that felt
like. *Those* feelings may be the kind that others of different social
characteristics are feeling right now in your group. You need not be
feeling them *at that moment* to understand how and why you should
be the one to take the first steps to overcome such feelings. Such a process, instead of creating a posture of "brotherhood" or "sisterhood"
that people will never really trust, usually leads to a softer yet more
consistent form of support, clear, individualized feedback, and your
own personal demonstrations of understanding. Don't first ask the
new Black member of your group about South Africa or Atlanta; see
what he or she thinks about Poland or city services. Don't ask a
woman if she is uncomfortable in a male-dominated group; instead,
you yourself raise suggestions to correct this domination. (And don't

nominate her to *chair* the subcommittee set up to look into the problem, unless she and other women want it!)

This kind of scrutiny, both personal and collective, is as necessary a feature of grass-roots organizations as is the work involved in maintaining democratic structures and procedures. It can be full of anguish because we know we *shouldn't* feel and don't want to behave in biased ways. If we can accept what we do, then we are simply accepting the otherwise easily acknowledged fact that we do not stand outside history but are always a part of it, for good and bad.

What makes grass-roots organizations so wonderful is that they form an arena where our potential to create that history is much greater than elsewhere. Despite all the racism, sexism, and class bias, there are groups in which we can actively attempt to erase that bias. For all our old behaviors, we are engaged in new ones that carry the outlines of behaviors quite different from the past. The "democratic experiment" discussed in history books is lived by grass-roots organizations in the tempestuous, difficult, and often winding ways that history demands. Being *alive,* the work then wondrously transforms itself from "experiment"—with all the well-ordered, controlled, and unreal borders that word implies—to the actual *democratic experience* it is. And where else today can you or I gain such experience to use throughout our lives?

NOTES

1. See Harry Braverman, *Labor and Monopoly Capital* (New York: Monthly Review Press, 1972).

2. Paulo Freire, *Pedagogy of the Oppressed* (New York: Seabury Press, 1971), especially Chapter 2.

3. This combination of "breaking down" and "creating" new standards is part of what makes so many grass-roots meetings so exhausting; seeming peaks and valleys are traveled each night. People don't simply "arrive" at a new set of beliefs, but must work through, often again and again, old ideas, attitudes, and behaviors while seeking and discovering untapped and perhaps barely perceived talents and abilities. Such circuitous travels *are* tiring, but they can be a magnificent journey!

4. Freire, *Pedagogy,* Chapter 1.

EXERCISES: TO FIGHT RACISM,
SEXISM, AND CLASS BIAS IN YOUR GROUP

1a. Review a previous interaction that revealed vestiges of your own racism, sexism, or class bias. Write what happened to you—both your *initial* feelings and your eventual *behavior*.

_____

_____

_____

_____

1b. What, specifically, exists in your social world that perpetuates those kinds of feelings? Anything recently? Or is it based on other, more subtle forms of socialization, family interactions, and the like?

_____

_____

_____

_____

1c. Without denying the feelings you have, what are some other behaviors you could use next time to counteract such problems? Are they realistic or do they bend too far in the opposite direction—are you feeling guilty rather than directing your energy positively?

_____

_____

1d. What can you do in your daily life to begin correcting deep-seated problems?

_____

_____

1e. If you responded to this exercise by feeling the "ism" lay in others and not yourself, why not take another issue of the three (or ageism or biases against the handicapped or a religious group) and ask these questions again. After all, no one is that pure!

_____

_____

2a. Identify some set of circumstances in your life where you felt left out, stereotyped, ostracized, or objectified. What did that feel like *in terms of your behavior with others*—angry, withdrawn, more guarded?

_____

_____

_____

_____

2b. Now identify what actions you would have appreciated (or did appreciate) from others that would have relieved your sense of objectification and your resulting behaviors in that circumstance. Likewise, note behaviors that bothered you the most.

_____

_____

_____

2c. Imagine that there are similar feelings felt by others every day, often in your presence (but not necessarily because of anything you yourself have done—the social circumstances may have created those feelings before you ever arrived). What can you do consistently to relieve those negative feelings?

_____

_____

_____

_____

Chapter 9

THE YEARS AHEAD

The years ahead are not going to be easy ones for grass-roots organizations. But we should not be lulled into inactivism by the illusion of either easy victory or the impossibility of success. Both the 200,000-person Labor Day March in New York and the equally impressive AFL-CIO civil rights demonstration on September 19, 1981, testify to the resevoir of potential mobilization that exists in every workplace and throughout every community. It is our job to face present conditions realistically, mobilizing the resources that do exist and generating maximum political capital from every meeting held and each strategy implemented. Our smaller actions of today in no small way prepare us for the larger movements of tomorrow—such as today's disarmament movement. While not always easy to accept, this recognition of our present role in building for the future is important to hold on to *and to respect.* Without grass-roots activists and organizations, however trim our sails and modest our present efforts, the future really would be worse.

This role recognition is part of how we learn to draw political satisfaction from the manner in which we do our work. As this book has consistently emphasized, developing leaders, democratically arriving at decisions, and confronting and dealing with racism and sexism are extremely important political acts. We can use these less tumultuous times to learn how to incorporate such organizing principles before we get swept away in later tides of intense activism—activism that will be less effective if such process issues are ignored today.[1]

The upsurge in activity (if not success) that has occurred over the last few years has been caused by many factors, as Heather Booth noted recently.[2] The recognition that we are working for more than our own self-interests (without denying those interests, either), the ability to work toward multiracial and cross-occupational alliances, and the efforts of various organizations (especially churches committed to the "social gospel" and trade union locals with an active rank and file) are all mentioned by Booth as some of the most important reasons for this upsurge. It is clear that many lessons learned from the mistakes of the 1960s (when single-issue constituencies and often counterinstitutional politics were highly popular) have contributed to the successful, forward-looking, and more political growth of grassroots activity.

In all honesty, however, there is still a tremendous amount of infighting and petty interorganizational squabbling that undercuts the effectiveness of many, many groups today. Such problems will not go away if we simply wipe the slate clean every time a group goes under, assuming that organizations and their members somehow start fresh every time. They don't, and old wounds must be healed before strong alliances can and will be built. These problems are usually manifested in two distinct ways.

First, demoralization does set in when groups are not as effective as they would like to be. Instead of adopting the kind of modest framework suggested throughout this book regarding objectives and method of functioning, some activists, wanting to be part of a "real" change effort, turn inward. Instead of attacking the real causes of most organizations' problems today in some realistic fashion, they target those whom they (often unconsciously) feel they can still influence—their peers. Instead of channeling their efforts into a modest, externally focused campaign, people launch internally focused vendettas that may soothe their immediate ache for meaning but inevitably harm their group's potential.

Second, some members often mistakenly construe dominance over a very small amount of turf as more important than joint but less directly powerful partnership with others in a larger political scene. This occurs when some activists become so immersed in their own organizing efforts that *their world* becomes *the world.* Since jostling for power on a larger stage is unrealistic, why not assume jostling each other for leadership as the spokesperson or best-identified group is not only realistic but necessary? If little serious attention is given in an ongoing way to the larger social reality surrounding our work (which would almost always place our work in a less grandiose perspective), then this search for individualized power becomes more tenable—even if irrelevant to the needs confronting our organizations today.

Underneath both these problems lies an insularity bred not only by organizational blinders but some political ones. I would argue that both sets of conflicts, while partially rooted in personal and organizational factors of any group, also flow from an unwillingness to grapple with the real economic and political realities of late twentieth-century American life. Implicit in each problem's origin is a political sense that the issue will still be positively dealt with, at least gradually, even while these forms of sectarianism occur. Such an assumption is based on the previous fifty years of American history: With varying cycles, a consistently expanding economy, coupled with a growing government, always made possible the improvement of material conditions for most Americans. While never adequate (and consistently racially, sexually, and class biased), this expansion meant that single-issue formations and grass-roots organizations would benefit—some housing would be built, better regulations would be passed, and so on. If in the midst of our fight to force government and business to "do more" such in-fighting occurred, there was enough success and enough material improvement to let one ignore such internal mistakes.

The late 1970s and early 1980s, however, have revealed how serious an error it would be to assume things will continue in the same, unilinear, gradually progressive way. The Reagan administration, backed by powerful economic and rightward political interests, has made this entirely clear as it slashes services and taxes in an attempt to right a decade-old economic crisis of international proportions.[3] When we recognize how serious are the economic problems and how entrenched is the opposition to our interests, turf battles and grandstanding move from the unnecessarily ineffective to the suicidal. To overcome these problems means to grapple with the serious economic and political issues of our time. They are many to look at, but three seem to stand out.

(1) What economic alternatives can we offer that communities can consider seriously to present rightward programs? The real popular strength of the Reagan administration's economic plan is that it establishes a clear and consistent alternative to the previous, liberal economic programs of the past that many people now perceive as

either irrelevant or harmful to their lives.[4] Whether that perception is "objectively correct" or not is secondary to the strength of that perception and the ensuing willingness of a broad spectrum of the American public to let "supply-side economics have a chance."[5] While many of us could easily critique the inflationary and socially disastrous consequences of supply-side economics, replete with wasteful defense overruns, inflationary tax cuts, and harmful "safety nets,"[6] few progressive alternatives have been put forth *concretely* for dealing with the kinds of economic problems faced by American industries—productivity, debt costs, plant relocations, runaway shops, and so forth—that do not simply echo the past. I am not suggesting the necessity of either blueprints or inherent political compromise before embarking on campaigns of opposition to present conservative plans. Such forms of either utopianism or wishful thinking are not helpful. But people must have clear and positive proposals that make sense to others if they are to rally behind them. Some remarkably effective alternatives to industrial layoffs have been proposed and successfully agitated for by England's Lucas Aerospace workers, followed by similar plans at a number of British, Italian, and French firms.[7] Positive agitational programs that are both winnable and directly counter to rightward assumptions about economic problems are not to be left to others, but must be mounted by grass-roots organizers, activists, and their organizations as well. If we are not as coherent and, to many whom we see as part of our constituencies, as original in our suggestions for economic revitalization, it is unlikely that we can expect to serve as a serious challenge to those currently in power.

(2) Grass-roots organizations must address seriously both the strengths and weaknesses of localism and, along with that analysis, reexamine various institutions that influence both local and national life.[8] Many grass-roots organizations know how important trade unions, religious groups (especially in Black communities) and established community organizations have to be in the building of solid coalitions strong enough to confront existing political arrangements.[9] What we must also do is examine the readiness and willingness of the leaders of these institutions actively to mobilize their memberships for social change. More than one commentator, including those hardly defined as radical,[10] have suggested that much of the present leadership of established progressive organizations has grown apart from their ranks, preferring to maintain closer relationships with figures once regarded as antagonistic to their groups' interests. They have thus come to fear mobilization as a threat to their own well-

crafted positions of power, preferring rhetorical gestures to actual mass-based commitment. The unwillingness of AFSCME DC 37's avowedly socialist leader Victor Gotbaum to oppose Mayor Koch in the 1981 mayoral elections "because he can't be defeated" is an example of the rupture between the spoken word and the actual practice of many leaders to whom grass-roots organizers have previously looked for direction.

Likewise, the inherent tensions in only localized actions have existed throughout the last two decades and can no longer be ignored as budgets are slashed and states and regions compete with one another for funding. The lure of localism is that its campaigns are more concretely immediate and many of its issues seem more winnable in the short run; its basic flaw is that more and more issues are tied directly to national concerns that cannot be resolved within one town or one state, but instead relate to economic problems of plant relocation, unfair national taxes, national subsidies for particular interests, such as defense, that are geographically skewed but still national in scope, and so on. Unfortunately, much community organization has been tied to a political conception of its work that places national or class issues on a back burner with a very low flame. The ensuing parochialism has made many activists quite thoughtful and creative at the neighborhood and community level but ill-equipped to deal with the broader problems that face almost all grass-roots organizations today. We must take time to train ourselves in the serious political assessment of both localism and the institutions within the communities in which we work.

(3) I believe the third political issue that grass-roots organizers must assess is electoral politics. A tremendous amount of grass-roots organizing is based on at least partial electoral solutions. Such a strategic approach carries with it the inevitable need to align with the Democratic party, especially the left-liberal wing led by Michael Harrington, the Democratic Socialist Organizing Committee (DSOC). How much of this is a necessary progressive response and how much of it is a replacement for action that would be directed at fully mobilizing the rank and file within other institutions to transform them and thus lay the basis for a more radical, class-based political party is a question that must be debated if we are to advance in the coming years.[11]

All of these questions are not secondary theoretical issues to be analyzed in abstractly focused study groups that never relate to the rest of the world. Each of these three issues demands grappling with

theory, but they all rest on the concrete needs of grass-roots organizations today—needs that must shape our strategies for tomorrow.
Some grass-roots organizers, understandably impatient with the slow
pace of our present movements and enraged at the growing injustice
around us, may wish to push these matters aside for "later." Unfortunately, these same items for analysis were on the grass-roots agenda
a decade ago, and "later" has now arrived—with a vengeance. It is
not enough to feel right and to fight against injustice. We must have a
pervasive, flexible analysis of our grass-roots organizing that can
shape our work in a clearer and more self-confident fashion for not
only immediate tactical needs but also long run, more politically
strategic matters that give shape to entire social movements.

If we engage in this analysis with a spirit of open comradeship and
support for our fellow activists, recognizing that it is more important
to discuss these issues substantively than it is to "win" a quickly
forgotten debate, we may well be on our way to joining theory and
practice in our daily lives in a manner that makes politics come alive
with meaning and purpose. After all, the vision of a better world that
we grass-roots organizers embrace is special, for it includes masses of
people enjoying the fruits of their labor and the creativity of collective
effort. This makes us quite distinct from those burdened with the
weight of elitism, where only the elect few can decide how the world is
run for all the rest of us.

That said, having such a wonderful vision should not interfere with
our recognition that it needs even more refining. By learning how to
move our groups ahead in the 1980s' conservative climate, by recognizing that the way we do our work is a source of political satisfaction
and purpose, and by willingly grappling with the complex but unavoid-
able economic and social issues of our time without succumbing to
either "vanguardism" or demoralization, we can all play a genuinely
important role today. For our work, no matter how small its present
focus and difficult its tasks, is laying the basis for a world far better
than others would allow. Quite simply, grass-roots organizing can
never be easy, but it offers a much better way to live!

NOTES

1. Paulo Freire's *Pedagogy of the Oppressed* (New York: Seabury Press, 1972) is
especially important as a political methodology that explains these issues in a demanding but totally realistic manner that any grass-roots organizer must grapple with. See

also Steve Burghardt, *The Other Side of Organizing* (Cambridge, MA: Schenkman, 1981), for an adaptation of Freire's ideas to the American scene.

2. "Interview with Heather Booth," *Social Policy,* September/October 1981, pp. 30-33.

3. See the Spring 1981 double issue of *Radical America,* Vol. 15, Nos. 1 and 2, for a thorough analysis of the Right and the so-far inadequate response by the progressive movements to counter the Right's powerful program. For those wishing to study the economic crisis, there is much to turn to. Try James J. O'Connor's *Fiscal Crisis of the State* (New York: St. Martin's Press, 1973) and, for an introductory overview, Edwards, Reich, and Weisskopf (eds.), *The Capitalist System* (New York: Prentice-Hall, 1978).

4. *Radical America, op. cit.*

5. *New York Times,* "Poll Finds Growing Acceptance of Public Even After Budget Cuts," August 12, 1981.

6. Steve Burghardt and Michael Fabricant, "The 'New American Plan' of Reindustrialization: Imagining Social Cuts Without Social Costs," National Association of Social Workers Annual Conference, Philadelphia, November 1981.

7. Dave Albury "Alternative Plans and Revolutionary Strategy," *International Socialism.* Vol. 2, No. 6, pp. 85-96.

8. The entire issue of *Social Policy,* 1979, Vol. 10, No. 2, is devoted to various issues of grass-roots and neighborhood organizing and is well worth the reading. See also Richard Margolis, "The Limits of Localism," *Working Papers,* 1981, Vol. 8, No. 4, pp. 32-40.

9. "Booth," *op. cit.*

10. Richard Shepherd, "Labor's Crisis in 1981," *New York Times,* September 8, 1981, p. 33.

11. Simply raising this issue may make my bias seem obvious, but I think it is important to analyze further the question of electoralism by analyzing the history and development of the Polish Solidarity movement. Its work did not begin inside the Communist Party—an avowedly "working-class party" which controlled the state itself!—but was based on the creation of its own independent trade union organizations. The eventual repurcussions to their transformed union base *included* a beginning transformation of the Communist Party itself. However, the process developed *from* the independently established rank-and-file unions *to* the Party, not the reverse. The power generated from its own autonomous position, rather than being either coopted or disoriented through internal Party actions, has maintained the pressure on the Party to continue the remarkable social and political transformation of Polish society—a transformation thought impossible three years ago. We need to study these lessons contemporary Polish history to see how much of Poland's experience is capable of replication here, especially as we consider electoral politics. For interesting material on Poland, see *Against the Current,* Vol. 1, No. 2, for a series of interesting articles on the potential and the problems of the Solidarity movement and what we in the United States can learn from it. While recent events tragically underscore the problems of working-class self-activity in Eastern Europe, the continuing Polish resistance still suggests that the future is not predetermined.

BIBLIOGRAPHY

ORGANIZING LITERATURE

Saul Alinsky, *Reveille for Radicals* (Chicago: University of Chicago Press, 1969); *Rules for Radicals* (New York: Vintage Books, 1972). The two standard classics by the best-known militant pragmatist.

Harry Boyte, *The Backyard Revolution: Understanding the New Citizen Movement* (Philadelphia: Temple University Press, 1980). Descriptively up-to-date presentation of the varied organizing efforts throughout the 1970s, although marred by lack of a clear, consistent analytic framework.

Steve Burghardt, *The Other Side of Organizing* (Cambridge, MA: Schenkman, 1982). A new formulation of organizing methodology that attempts to show that "how" we work is fraught with political implications.

Fred Cox, John Erlich, Jack Rothman, and John Tropman, *Strategies of Community Organization* (Itasca, IL: Peacock, 1979). The best traditional community organization reader in the field.

Farrell Dobbs, *Teamster Rebellion* (New York: Pathfinder Press, 1971). An excellent case study of rank-and-file trade union organizing, strategy, and tactics.

Joan Flanagan, *The Grass Roots Fundraising Book* (Washington, DC: The Youth Project, 1977). Good how-to-fund raise notebook for community-based fund raising.

Paulo Freire, *Pedagogy of the Oppressed* (New York: Seabury Press, 1972). Brilliant methodology concerned with the process of the practitioner-community member relationship. A must!

Andre Gorz, *Strategy for Labor* (Boston: Beacon Press, 1967). A highly popular, radical, left-social democratic analysis of how to create meaningful change in non-revoluntionary periods.

Marcia S. Joslyn-Scherer, *Communication in the Human Services* (Beverly Hills, CA: Sage, 1980). Helpful plan for human service activists for how to publicize events, improve communication, do newsletters, and so on.

Si Kahn, *How People Get Power* (New York: McGraw-Hill, 1970). A classic description of progressive organizing in rural and small-town communities.

Armand Lauffer, *Grantsmanship* (Beverly Hills, CA: Sage, 1978). A highly useful guide to the art and politics of grant writing.

Marcel Liebman, *Leninism Under Lenin* (London: Macmillan, 1979). The best analysis of the entire strategy and tactics of Lenin while he lived; a must for Marxists and social democrats.

John Tropman, *Effective Meetings* (Beverly Hills, CA: Sage, 1979). A good guide to the running of more traditional meetings.

PERIODICALS THAT CONSISTENTLY DISCUSS AND ANALYZE ORGANIZING STRATEGY

Against the Current
45 West 10th Street
New York, NY 10011

New, highly thoughtful Marxist magazine concerned with rank-and-file and community issues in the United States and abroad.

Catalyst: A Socialist Journal of the Social Services
P.O. Box 1144
Cathedral Station
New York, NY 10025

Consistently improving and wide-ranging magazine (embracing many different perspectives) on issues of primary concern to human service workers.

c/o: Journal of Alternative Human Services
1172 Morena Blvd.
San Diego, CA 92110

Reform and social democratic analyses of human service issues and community coalition actions; strong West Coast emphasis.

In These Times
Institute for Policy Studies
1509 N. Milwaukee
Chicago, IL 60622

Mainstream social democratic analysis of electoral politics, community, and trade union issues of the day.

Labor Notes
P.O. Box 20001
Detroit, MI 48220

Progressive rank-and-file-oriented newsletter on the American labor movement. A must for trade union activists.

NACLA
National Congress on Latin America
151 West 19th Street
New York, NY 10011

Thoughtful presentation of strategy on many Latin American affairs; social democratic and Marxist in orientation.

Radical America
Alternative Education Project
38 Union Square
Somerville, MA 02143

Solid reputation for analyzing long-term implications of various social movements; both social democratic and Marxist analyses.

Social Development Issues
University of Iowa
School of Social Work
Iowa City, IA 52242

Progressive, reform, and open
journal concerned with social
development in both urban and
rural areas.

Social Policy
33 West 42nd Street
New York, NY 10036

Reform and social democratic
analyses of neighborhood and
grass-roots organizing efforts.

Socialist Review
4228 Telegraph Avenue
Oakland, CA 94609

Left-social democratic journal
concerned with theoretical issues
underlying many social movements.

Working Papers
186 Hampshire Street
Cambridge, MA 02139

Reform-social democratic magazine
that emphasizes trade union and
working people's issues.

ORGANIZING NEWSLETTERS

The Citizens Advocate
Massachusetts Fair Share
304 Boylston Street
Boston, MA 02116

Community Jobs
The Youth Project
1704 R Street
Washington, DC 20009

Health-Pac
17 Murray Street
New York, NY 10008

People & Energy
Citizens Energy Project
1413 K Street N.W.
Washington, DC 20005

*Shelterforce: A National
Housing Publication*
380 Main Street
East Orange, NJ 07018

Sun Times
Solar Lobby
1001 Connecticut Avenue N.W.
Washington, DC 20036

USA
ACORN
628 Baronne
New Orleans, LA 70013

RESOURCES

The following organizations have many issue-specific pamphlets and monographs. Write to them for details.

ORGANIZING SCHOOLS

Center for Urban Encounter (CUE)
3410 University Avenue S.E.
Minneapolis, MN 55414

Education Center for Community Organizing (ECCO)
c/o Hunter College School of Social Work
129 East 79th Street
New York, NY 10021

Highlander Research and Education Center
Rt. 3, Box 370
New Market, IN 37820

Industrial Areas Foundation (IAF)
675 W. Jericho Turnpike
Huntington, NY 11743

National Training and Information Center
1123 W. Washington Blvd.
Chicago, IL 60607

New England Training Center for
  Community Organizers
19 Davis Street
Profidence, RI 02908

Organize Training Center
1208 Market Street
San Francisco, CA 94110

Pacific Institute for Community Organization
3814 East 14th Street
Oakland, CA 94601

The Institute
628 Baronne
New Orleans, LA 70113

NATIONAL NETWORKS FOR COMMUNITY ORGANIZING

Monitor
Center for Community Change (CCC)
1000 Wisconsin Avenue N.W.
Washington, DC 20007

*The Center for Community Economic
Development Newsletter*
Center for Community Economic Development
639 Massachusetts Avenue
Cambridge, MA 02139

Ways and Means
Conference/Alternative State
and Local Policies
2000 Florida Avenue N.W.
Washington, DC 20009

Just Economics
Movement for Economic Justice
1738 T Street N.W.
Washington, DC 20009

National Center for Economic
Alternatives (NCEA)
2000 P Street, Suite 200
Washington, DC 20036

Interchange
National Congress for Community
Economic Development (NCCELD)
1029 Vermont Avenue N.W.
Washington, DC 20036

Neighborhood Women
National Congress of Neighborhood
Women (NCNW)
11-29 Catherine Street
Brooklyn, NY 11211

AGenda: A Journal of Hispanic Issues
National Council of La Razza (NCLA)
1725 Eye Street N.W.
Washington, DC 20006

Disclosure
National People's Action (NPA)
1123 West Washington Blvd.
Chicago, IL 60607

Self-Help Reporter
National Self-Help Clearinghouse
33 West 42nd Street, Room 1227
New York, NY 10036

Ruralamerica
Rural America
1346 Connecticut Avenue N.W.
Washington, DC 20036

The Youth Project
1555 Connecticut Avenue N.W.
Washington, DC 20036

ABOUT THE AUTHOR

Steve Burghardt, MSW, Ph.D., teaches community organization and urban practice at the Hunter College School of Social Work in New York. An activist since the 1960s, he has spent the last eight years working in trade union and community coalitions, especially with public service workers and community groups fighting cutbacks. Author of numerous articles on organizing and the economic crisis, his books include *Tenants and the Urban Housing Crisis* (editor; Dexter, MI: New Press, 1972) and *The Other Side of Organizing* (Cambridge, MA: Schenkman, 1982). He currently is working with others in the creation of a Human Services Activists' Network and a Community Organizing and Resource Institute in New York City.